DOMESTIC MINOR
SEX TRAFFICKING

DOMESTIC MINOR SEX TRAFFICKING

BEYOND VICTIMS AND VILLAINS

ALEXANDRA LUTNICK

COLUMBIA UNIVERSITY PRESS • NEW YORK

Columbia University Press
Publishers Since 1893
New York   Chichester, West Sussex

Copyright © 2016 Columbia University Press
All rights reserved

Library of Congress Cataloging-in-Publication Data
Lutnick, Alexandrea
Domestic minor sex trafficking : beyond victims and villains / Alexandrea Lutnick
pages   cm
Includes bibliographical references and index.
ISBN 978-0-231-16920-2 (cloth : alk. paper) — ISBN 978-0-231-16921-9 (pbk. : alk. paper) —
ISBN 978-0-231-54083-4 (ebook)
1. Teenage prostitution—United States. 2. Human trafficking—United States.
3. Prostitutes—Services for—United States. 4. Social work with prostitutes—United States I. Title
HQ144.L96 2015
306.740835
2015014570

Columbia University Press books are printed on
permanent and durable acid-free paper.
This book is printed on paper with recycled content.
Printed in the United States of America

c 10 9 8 7 6 5 4 3 2 1
p 10 9 8 7 6 5 4 3 2 1

COVER DESIGN: Lisa Hamm

References to Internet Web sites (URLs) were accurate at the time of writing.
Neither the author nor Columbia University Press is responsible for URLs
that may have expired or changed since the manuscript was prepared.

For my parents, Carole and Carl Lutnick

CONTENTS

List of Illustrations and Tables   ix
Acknowledgments   xi

1. Introduction   1
2. Timing of Initiation: Routes Into and Reasons for
   Involvement in Sex Trades   14
3. Linked Lives: Third Parties, Violence, and
   Transitions in Involvement   27
4. Service Needs and Microsystem Challenges   47
5. Mesosystem Challenges: Interactions Between
   Case Managers and Other Systems   59
6. From Criminalization to Decriminalization: Local Responses to
   Domestic Minor Sex Trafficking   75
7. Macrosystem Challenges: The Impact of
   Policies and Culture   97
8. Conclusion   111

Appendix A: Study Site Information   123
Appendix B: Methodological Process   128
Appendix C: Case Narrative Interview Guide   134
Appendix D: Qualitative Analysis Code List   137
Appendix E: Sample Characteristics   140
Notes   149
References   155
Index   175

ILLUSTRATIONS AND TABLES

FIGURES

6.1.   Yearly U.S. prostitution arrest trends for minors by biological sex.   77

ApE.1.   Three programs' informal and formal client referral sources.   143

ApE.2.   Living situation(s) reported by clients at time of intake in the   144
three programs.

ApE.3.   Resources exchanged for sex reported by clients in the   146
three programs.

ApE.4.   Types of force, fraud, or coercion experienced in connection   147
with sex trades reported by clients in the three programs.

TABLES

4.1.   Client-Identified Service Needs   48

6.1.   Ten-Year Prostitution Arrest Trends for Minors, 2000–2009   76

6.2.   Fourteen-Year Prostitution Arrest Trends for Minors,   76
2000–2013

6.3.   Ten-Year Prostitution Arrest Trends for Minors by Sex,   77
2000–2009

ApE.1.   Sample Characteristics   141–42

ApE.2.   Sex Trade Characteristics   145

ApE.3.   Case Narrative Sample Characteristics   148

ACKNOWLEDGMENTS

I want to express my deep gratitude to all the people who have been integral to the completion of this book. Looking back over fifteen years, I am eternally grateful for the time I spent working at the St. James Infirmary, a peer-based occupational health and safety clinic for sex workers. How I think about the issue of young people who trade sex is directly informed by my time there as well as by my experiences working on studies with young people and adults who trade sex and working in a homeless family shelter. Being a part of the recent research team at RTI International that conducted a process evaluation of three programs funded by the U.S. Department of Justice to work with young people who trade sex was crucial to this book. My conversations with case managers and program staff at the Standing Against Global Exploitation (SAGE) Project in San Francisco, the STOP-IT Program of the Salvation Army in Chicago, and the Streetwork Project at Safe Horizon in New York City about the young people they work with and their experiences doing this work formed the foundation of this book. I thank all the staff, volunteers, clients, and research participants I have had the pleasure of interacting with. I hope that in this book I have represented the complexities of this issue that they have shared with me over the years.

My research for this book started out in the School of Social Welfare at the University of California–Berkeley. I can think of no other academic program that attracts such supportive individuals. Jennifer Lawson, Bryn King, Heliana Ramirez, Kelly Whitaker, Christina Branom, Wendy Wiegman, Leah Jacobs, Sarah Accomazzo, and Eve Ekman made what could have been a very stressful experience one of mutual support and learning. I especially thank Jae Sevelius, Julianna Deardorff, Jill Duerr Berrick, and in particular Eileen Gambrill. Working with Eileen has been one of the highlights of my experiences in the School of Social Welfare, and I am indebted to her for all the support and inspiration she provided. I also thank Samantha Majic for encouraging me to apply to a Ph.D. program. None of this would have happened if she had not given me the firm yet friendly nudge to just get over myself and take the GRE.

I have also been fortunate to work with an amazing group of people at RTI International. The opportunity to work with, learn from, and be supported by Alex Kral, Jennifer Lorvick, Megan Comfort, Lynn Wenger, Cindy Changar, Andrea Lopez, Christina Powers, Alexis Martinez, and Michèle Thorsen has been a gift. I was fortunate to be tapped by Deborah Gibbs to join her on the process-evaluation team. Without being part of that study, I would not have written this book. I thank Deborah Gibbs, Shari Miller, Jennifer Hardison Walters, and Marianne Kluckman for ongoing discussions about this topic and for graciously letting me carve out a piece of our study for this book.

Sometimes in life we are in the right place at the right time. I am deeply appreciative that Jennifer Perillo, the editor for social work, psychology, and criminology at Columbia University Press, happened to attend a presentation I gave at the Society for Social Work and Research Annual Conference. It was because of that chance meeting that the process of getting this book published began. Jenn has been encouraging from the beginning, and her enthusiasm for making this book happen has been humbling. I am also grateful to the anonymous peer reviewers who reviewed my proposal and final manuscript. I benefitted tremendously from their comments, insights, and critiques. Special thanks to Stephen Wesley for his help getting the manuscript ready for production and to Annie Barva for her editing of the final draft.

I consider myself very fortunate to be part of a community of people who identify as sex workers, survivors, scholars, activists, academics, service providers, or some combination of these various identities. In addition to the people I already mentioned, I also want to acknowledge the importance of Minh Dang, Carol Leigh, Stephany Ashley, Cyd Nova, Johannah Westmacott, Kelli Dorsey, Paniz Bagheri, Emi Koyama, Minouche Kandel, Naomi Akers, Chuck Cloniger, Deborah Cohan, and Sienna Baskin. These people and many others not included in this incomprehensive list have taught me so much, linked me to key resources, shared perspectives with me about this issue, and offered support and encouragement along the way.

Finally, I am very grateful for the support provided by my family, friends, and former teachers—my brother, Jack, and grandmother, Beverly; friends such as Holly Clark, Glen Dentinger, Kay Clark, Lynn Rosenthal, Bill Simpson, Nadia Oka, and Alan Scherer; my high school teachers Steve Worful and Greg Hemesath and my undergraduate teachers James Leo Walsh and William Edwards. In their own unique ways, each helped me write this book. Throughout this entire process, I have been blessed to have Joseph Carouba by my side. Moving through the world with Joe is one of the greatest gifts of my life. Although both of my parents have passed, I know that without their love and support, I would not be where I am today. Not a day goes by that I don't think about them and reflect on how lucky I am to be the daughter of Carole and Carl Lutnick.

DOMESTIC MINOR SEX TRAFFICKING

1

INTRODUCTION

America is in the grip of a highly profitable, highly organized and high-
ly sophisticated sex trafficking business that operates in towns large and
small, raking in upwards of $9.5 billion a year in the U.S. alone by abduct-
ing and selling young girls for sex.

—J. W. WHITEHEAD, "AMERICA'S DIRTY LITTLE SECRET"

I n 2000, the United States Congress authorized the Victims of Trafficking
and Violence Protection Act, more commonly referred to as the Trafficking
Victims Protection Act (TVPA). Section 103.8 defines any U.S. citizen or
lawful permanent resident younger than eighteen who is involved in commercial sex acts as a victim of a severe form of trafficking in persons.[1] Under
the TVPA's definition of sex trafficking of domestic minors, there is no need
to establish force, fraud, or coercion. The definition also does not require
third-party involvement,[2] nor does it require any movement from one location to another.[3] An increase in public awareness of and services for domestic
minor victims of sex trafficking increased followed the passage of the TVPA.

The authorization and subsequent reauthorizations as the Trafficking
Victims Protection Reauthorization Act (TVPRA) of 2003, 2005,[4] 2008,[5]
and 2013,[6] coupled with claims that human trafficking is the fastest-growing
criminal enterprise (Californians Against Sexual Exploitation 2012; Walker-
Rodriquez and Hill 2011), make the trafficking of minors appear to be a new
social issue, but the only thing new about domestic minor victims of sex trafficking is the term. Young people's involvement in trading sex is a complex issue that has existed throughout history (Schwartz 2009). Dating back to the
late nineteenth century, charitable organizations fought to bring attention to
the trafficking of women and girls for sexual purposes and tried to create
mechanisms for tackling the problem at a variety of levels (Cree 2008).[7] Over
the past one hundred years in the United States, this issue has been referred
to as *white slavery, juvenile prostitution, survival sex, sex work, commercial*

sexual exploitation, modern-day slavery, and *sex trafficking.* Complicating discussions is the fact that these terms (save for *white slavery,* which is used for a specific historical context) are oftentimes used interchangeably to talk about this issue. Depending on the term used, the young people involved are viewed as victims or fully formed agents or both.

Throughout this book, I use the term *sex trades* to refer to the act of trading sex for some type of payment. When quoting sources who use different terms, I leave those terms unchanged. I have chosen to use *sex trades* as opposed to, say, *sex work, prostitution, commercial sexual exploitation,* or *trafficking* because it brings with it minimal assumptions about the young people in this population and their experiences. The reality is that most young people "never use the term *trafficking*" (E. Dalberg, personal communication, March 2, 2011). The same is true for the term *victim.* Therefore, I do not use the term *victim* to refer to these young people unless I am quoting or referring to material that uses it. Labeling them victims oversimplifies their lived experiences, is disempowering (Sherman 2012), and "functions as an implicit character assessment of the . . . individual instead of an assessment of the social circumstances" (Zimmerman 2013, 12).

Just as nothing is new about young people's involvement in sex trades, nothing is new about their construction as victims. The discourse of young people's victimhood dates back to the White Slave Traffic Act of 1910. More commonly referred to as the Mann Act, this legislation marks the first instance when a federal law was aimed at domestic prostitution involving young cisgender women[8] and rendered their consent as immaterial (the term *cisgender* refers to those people whose gender identity matches their biological sex; the term *transgender* refers to those whose gender identity does not match their biological sex). The name "White Slave Traffic Act" was strategically used to evoke what "many believed was a serious and widespread practice: Commercial procurers taking innocent young girls and women by force and holding them captive with threats to their lives, a practice that resembled black servitude in its exploitative and barbarous nature" (Beckman 1984, 1112).

Introduced by Representative James R. Mann of Illinois, the White Slave Traffic Act provides that a person is guilty of violating the act if they "knowingly transport or cause to be transported,[9] or aid or assist in obtaining transportation for, or in transporting, in interstate or foreign commerce . . . any woman or girl for the purpose of prostitution or debauchery, or for any other immoral purpose, or with the intent and purpose to induce, entice, or compel such woman or girl to become a prostitute or to give herself up to debauchery, or to engage in any other immoral practice."[10] At this historical moment, a larger boundary crisis about women, sexuality, and the family appeared in response to industrialization and the move from rural to urban communities. This crisis reflected society's discomfort with women who were "urbanized and sexualized" (Brown 2008, 478) and raised uncertainty about where the boundary of acceptable and unacceptable behavior for women should be now that they were unattended outside of the home (Cohen 1972). The inclusion of the phrase "any other immoral purpose" in the text of the Mann Act reflects how the act sought to control women and girls' movement across state lines and to prohibit them from engaging in nonmarital sexual relations (Brown 2008). In his book *Panders and Their White Slaves* (1910), Clifford Roe defined white slavery as the "procuring, with or without their consent, girls and women for immoral houses and for lives of shame and detaining them against their wills until they have become so accustomed and hardened to lives of vice that they do not care to leave, become diseased, or too ashamed to face decent people again" (qtd. in Grittner 1990, 67). The removal of criteria of consent was critical to maintain the idea of white slavery. It would have been illogical to claim that someone who was a white slave had the capacity to give consent to her enslavement. In 1918, the Texas District Court offered the opinion that the purpose of the Mann Act was to "protect women who were weak from men who were bad" (qtd. in Grittner 1990, 155).

Enforcement of the Mann Act was expanded beyond its initial intent to prevent interstate prostitution and to protect women. In *Caminetti v. United States*,[11] two couples voluntarily traveled together from California to Nevada for the weekend. Because of the inclusion of "any other immoral purpose" in the legislative text, the Supreme Court ruled that even when no commercial intention or profit was present, the Mann Act applied to voluntary immoral acts (Beckman 1984), which these couples' weekend together was considered to be. In the 1915 case *United States v. Holte*,[12] Justice Holmes raised the need to "abandon the illusion that the woman always is the victim." Under this ruling, women could not be liable as an accomplice, but they could be tried as a conspirator. A conspiracy charge was deemed appropriate when the woman was considered a willing participant. The U.S. Federal Bureau of Investigation (FBI) is also responsible for the overexpansion of the Mann Act.

In a policy referendum it issued in 1949,[13] agents were encouraged to present to attorneys cases "that alleged interstate transportation but failed to indicate the existence of prostitution" (Beckman 1984, 1124). In these cases, women were charged with conspiracy and held in custody in hopes of getting them to testify against the men who transported them.

The Mann Act was used to prosecute individuals beyond the scope of its original intent of curtailing commercial vice. In an examination of 87 percent of the case records (n = 156) of women convicted and incarcerated for violating the Mann Act between 1927 and 1937, Marlene D. Beckman (1984) found that 23 percent of the examined cases involved women who traveled with their boyfriends across state lines when one or both of them were married to someone else. In these cases, both the woman and man were arrested as co-conspirators after they were turned in by the man's wife. In 16 percent of the cases, the women's involvement in trading sex was secondary to their interstate travel with a boyfriend or husband. These women engaged in prostitution only to earn enough money to complete their travels. Fifteen percent of the women were regularly involved in trading sex to support themselves and were arrested when they solicited at a hotel across state lines. Most represented in the cases reviewed (46 percent) were women who identified as prostitutes and were arrested for aiding or securing transportation for another woman to cross state lines for prostitution. These cases present a very different image than the one of women and girls abducted and forced to trade sex, and they illustrate how the Mann Act became a mandate for prosecuting women who "were an affront to traditional American values" (Brown 2008, 478).

THE NUMBERS GAME

The number of young people who currently trade sex is unknown. A "woozle effect" (Gelles 1980) has taken place whereby the methodologically flawed guesstimate by Richard Estes and Neil Weiner (2005) that between 100,000 and 300,000 young people are at risk for involvement in sex trades has subsequently been cited by politicians, journalists, academics, and activists as the number of youth in the United States who trade sex (Stransky and Finkelhor 2008). Along the way, the descriptor *at risk* fell off, and for many this number has become the true prevalence of youth involved in sex trades in the United States, despite the fact that not all young people who are considered "at risk" will go on to trade sex. A further complication with the number provided by Estes and Weiner is that it is based on fourteen speculative and nonexclusive categories of at-risk young people (i.e., gang members, runaways, those living along the U.S.–Canada or U.S.–Mexico border). What this means is if someone fits into multiple categories, he or she will be counted multiple times. Academics and some mainstream media sources have refuted the Estes and Weiner number (see, e.g., Cizmar, Conklin, and Hinman 2011; Fedina 2014; Koyama 2011b; Pinto 2011; Stransky and Finkelhor 2008). David Finkelhor, director of the Crimes Against Children Research Center, explained additional problems with the Estes–Weiner number: "As far as I'm concerned, [Estes and Weiner's study] has no scientific credibility. That figure was in a report that was never really subjected to any kind of peer review. It wasn't published in any scientific journal" (qtd. in Cizmar, Conklin, and Hinman 2011).

Other numbers have been put forth to estimate the scope of this issue. In a nationally representative study of 13,294 young people in grades 8 through 12, 3.5 percent ($n = 465$) reported ever exchanging sex for drugs or money (Edwards, Iritani, and Hallfors 2006, 355). One limitation of this finding is the possibility that someone who paid for sex could also respond affirmatively to this item. In a subsequent wave of this study, the National Longitudinal Study of Adolescent Health, this limitation was addressed, and the question about involvement in trading sex was divided into one question about selling and another question about buying sex. Of the 12,240 young people ages eighteen through twenty-six surveyed in this study, 245 (2 percent) began buying and the same number began selling sex between Wave I and Wave III of the study (Kaestle 2012, 317). The data do not indicate how many reported both buying and selling. They also do not indicate at what age the person started trading sex; the individual may or may not have started before he or she turned eighteen. The findings are also limited to those who were in school when the survey was administered. However, if we can believe that 2 percent of school-age young people (thirteen to seventeen years old) in the United States have traded sex at least once, based on the 2010 U.S. census this percentage amounts to 423,536 young people (U.S. Census Bureau 2014).

Crime data are another source that can be used to assess the scope of young people's involvement in sex trades. One source of crime data is the

Uniform Crime Reports (UCR) published by the FBI. Because not all young people who trade sex are arrested and/or charged for prostitution offenses, these data are limited. Likewise, the data do not indicate how many of the total arrests are one-time occurrences and how many represent multiple arrests of the same individual. With those limitations acknowledged, the data indicate that 550 young people were arrested in 2013 for prostitution-related offenses (U.S. FBI 2014a). The other source of crime data is the National Incident-Based Reporting System (NIBRS), which is part of the UCR. Section 237 of the 2008 TVPRA mandated that the FBI classify human trafficking as a Part I crime in the UCR and a Group A offense in the NIBRS. As a consequence, in 2013 the FBI started collecting data about two categories of human trafficking for the UCR: (1) commercial sex acts, where force, fraud, or coercion is used or where the person performing the acts has not attained eighteen years of age; and (2) involuntary servitude, which does not include commercial sex acts. A review of the data from 2013 shows that six human-trafficking incidents were reported. All of the crime victims were identified as female, and all but one were younger than eighteen.[14] The data did not differentiate between the two categories of trafficking.

It is clear that it is not possible to know the exact number of young people who are involved in sex trades. Lists of all youth in the United States who trade sex do not exist, which prevents any type of random sampling. An additional complication is that young people have many good reasons for not acknowledging their involvement, such as concerns about being judged, stigmatized, or arrested. Based on the previous examination of some of the more commonly cited prevalence data, we see how the numbers range wildly from 5 to 423,536. In a systematic review of forty-two published books about human trafficking, Lisa Fedina (2014) found that 78 percent of the books cited prevalence data from at least one flawed source. This misuse of data is, of course, not limited to books. It can also easily be found in newspaper articles, news shows, documentaries, journal articles, activist claims, organizational literature, political speeches, and governmental hearings. Despite awareness about the flawed nature of these data, "current literature, media sources, and anti-trafficking campaigns and organizations continuously cite these problematic estimates and go as far as to claim that the reality of the problem is much greater than what the estimates project" (Fedina 2014, 2). To rely on unsupported estimates is a disservice to knowledge building and shifts the attention away from the social factors that create vulnerabilities among youth.

Just as the numbers vary about how many young people in the United States are involved in sex trades, so to do estimates about the age of first entry. Arriving at a consistent estimate of the age of first entry is complicated in that studies use different age eligibility criteria. Some studies use the U.S. Centers for Disease Control definition that specifies youth as between the ages of fourteen and twenty-four (Shannon et al. 2010); others define the period as ages fourteen to twenty-three (Haley et al. 2004; Tyler, Hoyt, and Whitbeck 2000); and still others extend it to age twenty-five or twenty-six (Chettiar et al. 2010; Marshall et al. 2010; Weber et al. 2002, 2004). Research about youth in the juvenile justice system focuses primarily on twelve- to seventeen-year-olds (Brown, Rodriguez, and Smith 2010; Halter 2010; Mitchell, Finkelhor, and Wolak 2010). Some studies focus on a particular period, such as from age fifteen to seventeen (Nadon, Koverola, and Schludermann 1998), whereas others rely on the federal definition of a child as anyone younger than eighteen (Curtis et al. 2008). Among these studies, the average age of entry typically falls between fifteen and seventeen.

Because the average age of entry ultimately depends on the age of the sample, studies that include older individuals have found the average age of entry into sex trades to be around twenty to twenty-two (Kramer and Berg 2003; Lutnick and Cohan 2008; Martin, Hearst, and Widome 2010; McClanahan et al. 1999). One study among adult women calculated the average age of entry for those who started before they were eighteen (average age at start = fifteen) and those who started after that (average age at start = twenty) (Martin, Hearst, and Widome 2010). If studies sample only young people, the average age will reflect that focus and will never be higher than eighteen. By including both sets of numbers, the set gathered from samples of young people and the set gathered from samples of their older counterparts, it is clear that not all people who trade sex start when they are young and that not all youth continue to trade sex past the age of eighteen (Edwards, Iritani, and Hallfors 2006; Martin, Hearst, and Widome 2010).

Despite the challenges of assessing the average age of entry, some work has suggested that age at entry does matter. A study of adult cisgender women in Chicago found that those who reported that they were younger than fifteen when they first traded sex had worse outcomes than those who were at least fifteen. The early starters were more likely to have run away from home, to have used drugs or alcohol as teens, and to have greater health problems as adults and were less likely to graduate from high school (Raphael and Shapiro 2002). Among a sample of cisgender women in Minneapolis, those women who reported trading sex as juveniles were more likely to have run away from home at some point and to have used drugs at an earlier age (although their first drug use typically happened after initiation into trading sex). This study also found that women who started before they were eighteen and who were still trading sex as adults traded sex more frequently and reported higher rates of street-based prostitution than those who started after age eighteen (Martin, Hearst, and Widome 2010). Research findings indicate that those who are involved in trading sex for longer periods of time are at an increased risk of experiencing violence and abuse (Cobbina and Oselin 2011).

The findings about the impact of age of first entry indicate that to approach people younger than eighteen as a unified category ignores the ways in which different age groups experience their involvement in sex trades. Programs, policies, and prevention efforts thus need to be targeted to those experiences that precede an individual's entry into sex trades.

THE HETEROGENEITY OF YOUNG PEOPLE WHO TRADE SEX

Young people who trade sex are not a homogenous group; all classes, races, genders, and sexualities are represented.[15] Although most media accounts of this issue focus only on cisgender girls, some research indicates that more cisgender boys than cisgender girls are involved (Dennis 2008; Finkelhor and Ormrod 2004; Greene, Ennett, and Ringwalt 1999; Kaestle 2012; Schaffner 2006), but other research has found that equal numbers of cisgender boys and girls are involved (Estes and Weiner 2005). When included in mixed-gender samples, transgender youth constitute about 8 percent of the study sample (Curtis et al. 2008). However, research that focuses specifically on young transgender women finds that approximately 60 percent will report having ever traded sex for some type of payment (Garofalo et al. 2006; Wilson et al. 2009). Literature about young transgender men engaged in sex trades is noticeably absent. Among the very few studies that look at transgender men who trade sex, the samples are composed solely of adults (Clements-Nolle et al. 2001; Sevelius 2009). Despite findings that cisgender boys and transgender youth are involved in trading sex at levels equal to or surpassing that of cisgender girls, the research literature focuses largely on cisgender girls. In a review of articles published in social science journals, Jeffrey P. Dennis (2008) found that of the fifteen articles that discussed young people specifically, ten focused only on cisgender girls, four on cisgender boys and girls, but only one exclusively on cisgender boys. None of the articles addressed transgender youth. Based on these numbers, cisgender girls are ten times more likley to be the focus of research. This erasure of transgender youth and cisgender boys is likely indicative of the ways in which the social construction of young cisgender girls positions them as especially vulnerable and in need of social and legal interventions.

The behaviors and settings of sex trades are as diverse as the young people involved in them. Behaviors range from engaging in survival sex (where the person trades sex to fulfill basic needs for food, clothing, and shelter) to being part of street-based sex trades, working in brothels, and performing in pornographic films. However, caution needs to be employed when interpreting these various terms. For example, the term *street based* does not necessarily mean that the sex act itself occurs on the street. It is frequently used in reference to the place where the young person and client connect, although the encounter is typically conducted at the client's apartment, at a hotel, or in a car. It is rare for young people in the United States to be part of an organized process where they are moved from one city to another to trade sex (Mitchell et al. 2011).

Narratives about white slavery issued prior to and after the implementation of the Mann Act are strikingly similar to those presented today about domestic minor sex trafficking. Writing about the Mann Act, Beckman discusses the ways in which "the Progressive Era reformers who supported the Act had used the words 'white slavery' to promote the vision of women held in bondage against their will, of mysterious druggings and abductions of helpless young girls" (1984, 1111). Since the passage of the TVPA in 2000, we have been inundated with "sensationalized stories" offered by mainstream media and antitrafficking activists about domestic minor sex trafficking (Lloyd 2012). Stories about young girls being abducted (*ABC News* 2006;

Amber 2010; Whitehead 2014), lured (*ABC News* 2006; Abdullah 2014; Callahan and Schroeder 2014; Covenant House 2014), forced (Do 2014; Khan 2010; Wang 2014; Whittier 2014), kidnapped (Saar 2010), enslaved or made into sex slaves (*ABC News* 2006; Holden 2013; Kaye 2007; Kristof 2013, 2014; Tucker 2013), and hooked on drugs by organized crime units (Holden 2013; Khan 2010) and by armed, violent pimps (Kaye 2007; Kristof 2011, 2014) have captured our collective imagination.

The aim of this book is to move past homogenous representations of this group of young people. By expanding the narrative beyond simplistic accounts of victims and villains, it will allow a more nuanced understanding of both this social issue and the young people involved to emerge. It presents a diverse, multisited picture of young people who trade sex as well as the experiences of case managers and other staff who work with them and examines the current policies relevant to this issue. Many different routes and motivations lead young people to trade sex, and the structural factors and inequalities that precede their involvement need to be examined. To develop and implement effective policies and programs, we must be willing to acknowledge the diversity of youth who trade sex, explore the ways in which our constructions of childhood and victimhood may contribute to the social marginalization of young people, and assess what we as a community can do to offer alternatives so that youth do not feel that sex trades are the only way they can meet their needs and wants. I argue that the approach of trying to get "the bad guys" has not brought about significant improvements for the young people these legal responses purportedly aim to protect. The TVPA's reclassification of this group of youth as victims, coupled with the reality that rigorous research is notably absent from much of the information about this topic issued by the U.S. media and government, has created a pressing need to reexamine this complex social issue. As Sienna Baskin, codirector of the Sex Workers Project at the Urban Justice Center, explains, "We can really care about human trafficking, and care about survivors of human trafficking, but [we] also need to be critical of that construct and think critically about it" (2014a).

The data in this book come from multiple sources. I use case history narratives about young people who trade sex. Over a twenty-two-month period, program staff at three community-based organizations—the Standing Against Global Exploitation (SAGE) Project in San Francisco, the STOP-IT

Program of the Salvation Army in Chicago, and the Streetwork Project at Safe Horizon in New York City—detailed the experiences of young people who trade sex. During semiannual site visits to the three agencies, I collected a total of forty-five unique narratives (fifteen from each site) and sixty-three updates (multiple updates for some individuals). Case managers are identified by name, but no identifiable information is provided about the young people with whom they work. I also incorporate material from conference proceedings, interviews with key informants, and published materials. (See appendixes A, B, C, D, and E for more detailed descriptions of the programs I worked with, my methods, and my findings.)

My analysis of all materials was guided by life course theory. This theory alerts us to the reality that people's behaviors and outcomes are the result of a dynamic process that involves the person, the environment, and time (Bronfenbrenner 1979; Elder 1994) and that their choices are contingent upon the opportunities and constraints of the social structure and culture (Elder 1998). What this means for young people who trade sex is that the structural factors that are antecedents to their involvement in commercial sex need to be examined. Initiation into commercial sex cannot be understood in isolation and does not warrant a one-size-fits-all approach (Godette, Headen, and Ford 2006). Rather, life course theory offers a framework that is broad enough to represent the heterogeneity of experiences among young people who trade sex. This spectrum includes those instances when youth are truly forced against their will to trade sex as well as the structural, social, and cultural contexts that precede young people's own decisions to become involved in sex trades. Likewise, it accounts for the experiences of some young people who "feel that the question of choice is irrelevant or more complicated than choice/no choice" (Iman et al. 2009, 7).

Guided by life course theory, chapters 2 and 3 examine the different routes and reasons that lead domestic youth to trade sex and the ways in which their experiences are linked to others. Instead of trying to understand their initiation in isolation, chapter 2 takes into consideration the structural and social contexts in which initiation occurs. In so doing, it finds that various factors such as fulfilling emotional needs, seeking gender and sexual identity affirmation, experiencing overt force, seeking sensation, running away from or getting pushed out of their homes, and being neglected contribute to young people trading sex. Chapter 3 examines how the lives of young people are lived interdependently, with their social ties to others channeling their actions and decisions. This chapter discusses third-party involvement and the types of relationships young people have with these people. With linked lives comes the potential for violence. Chapter 3 also describes the pervasive violence that young people who trade sex experience. It concludes with an examination of factors that influence the ways in which young people move in and out of involvement in trading sex. These two chapters counter the dominant narrative of young cisgender girls forced to trade sex by pimps with the more nuanced and complex realities of these young people's lives.

Just as there are a variety of young people who trade sex, these youth have a diversity of service needs. In chapters 4, 5, and 6, I use Urie Bronfenbrenner's (1979) ecological systems theory to describe the micro-, meso-, and macrolevel challenges of working with this population. Although some of the challenges in providing services for young people who trade sex parallel those of providing services for other high-risk youth, especially at the individual or microlevel, others are specific to working collaboratively with other agencies at the mesolevel. And some are a result of the ways in which the political and cultural contexts at the macrolevel limit the range of options available to young people. These chapters offer suggestions for addressing these challenges.

Because prostitution is regulated largely by the states and not by the federal government, the TVPA is limited in its applicability. To illustrate this discrepancy, chapter 7 starts with an examination of arrest rates since the enactment of the TVPA. As a consequence of the discrepancy, some young people are seen and treated as victims, some are arrested and treated like criminals, and others are "arrested for their own good" in an attempt to "protect" them (Baskin 2014b). This chapter also explores factors associated with the consideration of young people as victims. It then describes the local responses enacted in California, Illinois, and New York to address the issue of young people who trade sex. These three states offer the range of regulatory frameworks for sex trades that involve minors: criminalization, partial decriminalization, and decriminalization. They also have anti–human trafficking task forces, and two of the states (New York and Illinois) have vacatur remedies that allow people who are officially designated as victims of human trafficking to have prostitution-related offenses erased from their records.

After a presentation of these three models, I discuss the benefits and limitations of each approach, paying particular attention to the impact of criminalization and offer suggestions for how local responses can be revised to better meet these young people's needs.

The book concludes with a discussion about the importance of recognizing the diversity of young people who are involved in trading sex and their reasons for involvement in it. This final chapter reiterates how referring to these young people as victims ignores the resiliency that so many of them demonstrate and the fact that they are doing the best they can with limited options and limited support. The dominant narrative of pimp-controlled young cisgender women has resulted in the support of policies that are counterproductive. The collateral consequences of these policies have increased young people's vulnerabilities. I argue that based on our current approach to this issue, the United States is not yet committed to antioppression models of youth empowerment.

2

TIMING OF INITIATION

ROUTES INTO AND REASONS FOR INVOLVEMENT IN SEX TRADES

I t is rare for anti-trafficking campaigns to acknowledge the different routes and reasons that lead youth to trade sex (O'Connell Davidson 2005). The dominant narrative presented by these campaigns and portrayed in the media is that of a young cisgender girl forced to sell sex by an older cisgender man who is a pimp. Moving beyond this simplistic explanation, however, we find that a variety of factors influence how and why young people become involved in trading sex.

This chapter examines the precipitating factors that contribute to young people's becoming involved in trading sex. Some young people are housed, but their basic survival or emotional needs or both are not being provided for by the adults in their lives. Among young people who are homeless, trading sex becomes a strategy for survival. The structural violence that impacts lesbian, gay, bisexual, transgender, and queer (LGBTQ) youth contributes to their involvement in trading sex. For some of these young people, trading sex offers them the opportunity to have their gender and sexuality validated by others. This chapter also describes how young people trade sex because it provides for their basic needs, because they perceive it to be exciting, and because it gives them a way to buy material items they otherwise cannot afford. It also presents narratives of young people who are forced to trade sex and explores the role of drug use in initiation. The chapter ends with an examination of the association between sexual abuse and involvement in trading sex.

HOUSED BUT STILL NEEDING TO SURVIVE: THE ROLE OF NEGLECT

Trading sex to survive is a reality for many youth who are housed but whose basic survival needs for food and clothing are not provided or who have had to take on adult roles as providers for their siblings. In New York, a case manager described the way one client's adoptive mother did not provide for him: "She's not going to lock the door on him, but she's not doing much else besides leaving the door unlocked" (A. Kogel-Smucker, personal communication, May 22, 2012). Program staff explained situations where parents did not provide food or clothing for their children as well as instances when parents would move and leave their children behind without any means by which they could support themselves. In one such case, a young cisgender woman had been living with her father after her mother had abandoned them. Her father eventually entered a relationship with another woman and then moved out of state to live with her, leaving "[his daughter and her boyfriend] in the apartment with no money, no food or anything. He just stopped being in contact with her" (J. Skelton, personal communication, November 8, 2011). Speaking at the annual Freedom Network Conference, Dr. Meredith Dank, senior researcher at the Urban Justice Institute, recounted the reasons why young people who are housed begin to trade sex: "Some still live at home but because of familial poverty this is how they contribute to the rent, this is how they put food on the table. There were a number of young people we interviewed who were actually supporting their siblings and were the ones to buy clothing and food for their siblings" (2014).

FULFILLING EMOTIONAL NEEDS

Some young people trade sex to fulfill emotional needs that are not being filled elsewhere (Hanna 2002; Pierce 2012). Cheryl Hanna reflects that "most girls are not motivated by lust or greed or gluttony or wrath or envy or pride or sloth; they are lured by love. In that sense, they are no different, really, than many, many, teenage girls (and women) who look for it in all the wrong places" (2002, 3).

Case managers in San Francisco and Chicago report that some of their clients feel as if no one is there for them, that nobody loves them. These youth want their parents to comfort them (P. Bagheri, personal communication, October 19, 2011) and doubt whether any of their family members love them (N. Woodcox, personal communication, October 13, 2011). A clinical director in San Francisco described how losing an important relative left one young cisgender woman feeling emotionally neglected: "[She was] right around twelve years old; I think her uncle had gotten shot, and he was like the one that actually cared about her, and so here she lost somebody that really loved her . . . and she then recognized how she started needing to be loved, and she would walk down the street, and people would call out certain things to her, and it felt like she was being recognized and loved, and then she started to go into that world [of trading sex]" (R. Erwin, personal communication, May 25, 2012).

In such situations, the love and attention young people receive from clients or third parties contribute to their initial engagement in trading sex (Calvin 2010; Gragg et al. 2007). For some, this means coupling with people who pay them for sex. For others, it means forming an intimate relationship with somebody who over time asks, forces, or coerces them to trade sex. Sergeant Andre Bottoms of the Louisville Metro Police Department recounted the ways in which a young cisgender woman's emotional needs resulted in her becoming involved in trading sex: "From what I understand she was from a broken home, [there] wasn't a father figure in her life, mother worked all the time, she didn't really get a lot of attention. Met a guy that seemed to be very nice to her, showed her a lot of attention, bought her things, and then she kind of fell into that trap" (in Shaw 2013).

THE IMPACT OF HOMELESSNESS

Regardless of the reasons why young people leave or are pushed out of their homes, being homeless is associated with trading sex. Studies of street-based young people find that those who have ever traded sex are more likely to report histories of homelessness (Haley et al. 2004; Weber et al. 2004; Yates et al. 1991). Once homeless, youth have limited to no employment options. In addition, for a variety of reasons some young people prefer not to live in shelters, group homes, or foster homes. Because the law prevents all youth from entering into contracts such as rental agreements and some of them from obtaining employment without the consent of a parent or guardian, their options for housing and employment are severely restricted. These limitations, coupled with the absence of advancement opportunities for youth, increase the likelihood that they will consider trading sex to be their least-worst option for meeting their financial needs. Thus, poverty, homelessness, laws that govern a young person's ability to work, and the laws that place restrictions on the age at which a person can enter into a contract are all structural conditions that can result in trading sex as an economic strategy.

HOMOPHOBIA AND TRANSPHOBIA

The dominant narrative about young people involved in trading sex inaccurately depicts it as affecting only young, heterosexual, cisgender women and erases the experiences of LGBTQ youth. Because "LGBTQ youth face high rates of incarceration, family rejection, homelessness, [and] child welfare involvement, . . . [the] intersection of gender identity, housing insecurity, institutionalized homophobia and transphobia, conspire to make LGBTQ kids more vulnerable to being exploited" (Croce 2014). Several studies have found that sexuality and gender identities are associated with involvement in trading sex. Young people who identify as lesbian, gay, or bisexual, who report a romantic attraction to someone of the same sex, or who have engaged in sexual activity with someone of the same sex are more likely to have exchanged sex for some type of payment (Chettiar et al. 2010; Edwards, Iritani, and Hallfors 2006; Marshall et al. 2010; Weber et al. 2004). A survey of youth in six states found that LGB youth were more likely than heterosexual youth to trade sex (Van Leeuwen et al. 2006).

These findings are likely attributable to the reality that homophobic and transphobic living situations at home effectively push LGBTQ young people out of their homes and into the street economy (Quintana, Rosenthal, and Krehely 2010). The National Gay and Lesbian Taskforce Policy Institute found that one in four LGBT teens are forced to leave or run away from home, and approximately 20 to 40 percent of young people who are homeless identify as LGBT (Ray 2006). One case manager reported that when a young cisgender woman disclosed to her family that she was gay, her adopted mother told her, "You better say you're not, or you can't live here anymore" (E. Knowles Wirsing, personal communication, March 2, 2011). Another case manager explained how a young transgender woman left home because her family did not accept her gender identity: "The biggest thing with her was that . . . her family was not accepting of it [being transgender]. Her family was very religious; her adopted mother was a minister, and so was her adopted father, so they were really, really against it, and she lived in a community where transgenders were not welcome. So therefore . . . if her family didn't accept her, then she was still going to do it but away from home" (A. Velasquez, personal communication, October 31, 2011).

In addition to turning to sex trades as a means of survival while homeless, young transgender people initiate trading sex when transphobia limits or eliminates their employment options (Grant et al. 2011). In one study, more than half of the transgender women who trade sex reported that the inability to find gainful employment resulted in their turning to sex trades (Garofalo et al. 2006). This issue of limited economic opportunities was raised in focus groups with young people in New York City, where the transgender participants shared that the economic barriers that result because of their gender identity contribute to their entry into sex trades (Gragg et al. 2007). Involvement in sex trades often becomes a strategy employed to address some of the economic necessities in these young people's lives.

Some LGBTQ young people also trade sex to "live" their gender and sexuality (O'Connell Davidson 2005). In other words, young transgender women receive gender affirmation while trading sex (Garofalo et al. 2006; Wilson and Widom 2010). A case manager in Chicago described the experience of one transgender youth she worked with: "For the most part she said she loved what she did; she loved the fact" that clients considered her to be a woman (A. Velasquez, personal communication, October 31, 2011). Among young men who identify as gay, trading sex allows them to receive the sexual attention of other men and to explore their sexuality. Although an absence of literature exists about the sexual pleasure that young cisgender women may experience through sex trades, it is not uncommon for research focusing on young cisgender men and transgender individuals to cite that they experience sexual pleasure with some of their clients (Estes and Weiner 2005). A case manager in New York relayed a conversation with a young cisgender man who reported that what he found exciting about trading sex was "the drug use and meeting new people and sex" (A. Kogel-Smucker, personal communication, May 22, 2012).

DESIRES AS OPPOSED TO NEEDS

Rather than engaging in sex trades for survival, some young people report trading sex because they are drawn to what they perceive as an exciting lifestyle (Cates 1989; Cobbina and Oselin 2011; Gray 1973). As early as 1973, young cisgender women reported that they became involved in trading sex because they considered it "glamorous" (Gray 1973, 410). A young cisgender woman interviewed by Jennifer Cobbina and Sharon Oselin reported that she started trading sex as a young person "because of the money [and] the excitement" (2011, 321). These young people are housed and have all of their basic needs provided for them. A case manager in San Francisco described the background of one such young person: "Her living situation, it's very good. They live in a very nice area; she's very provided for, has all the necessities and then some" (S. Larrea, personal communication, October 18, 2011). For others, trading sex gives them access to luxury items such as jewelry and video games (Adler 2003; Cates 1989; Estes and Weiner 2005). Young cisgender women report trading sex because "someone's going to buy [them] some really expensive jewelry or something [they] don't need" (J. Westmacott, personal communication, March 23, 2011). In these instances, it is their desires as opposed to their needs that motivate young people to trade sex. One young cisgender man "initially got involved just because there were some older guys on his block who just were kind of cruising him and initially were just like, 'Well, we can give you nice stuff, nice things'" (J. Villarin, personal communication, March 23, 2011).

SUPPORT DRUG USE

The findings about the role of drug use in initiation of sex trades are inconsistent. Some research has found that drug addiction can precede initiation of trading sex (Marcus and Curtis 2013; Warf et al. 2013). Other research, such as the work by Cobbina and Oselin (2011) and the data from my interviews with program staff, does not find that a large portion of young people start trading sex to support a drug habit. In Cobbina and Oselin's (2011) study, among the seventeen cisgender women who started trading sex before the age of eighteen, none started trading sex to sustain their drug use. Of the forty-five case narratives I conducted with case managers, only two were about young people who started trading sex to support their drug use. In one of those two cases, the young cisgender woman told her case manager that her mom provided her with everything she needed, but she was trading sex because she wanted access to drugs (N. Woodcox, personal communication, April 25, 2012).

OVERT FORCE

Noticeably absent from the larger research literature and from the case history narratives I collected is the story most represented in the media: youth forced by a stranger into trading sex. Based on the findings from both my work and that of others (Curtis et al. 2008; Marcus and Curtis 2013; Marcus, Horning, et al. 2014; Warf et al. 2013), it appears that up to 10 percent of young people are forced by someone to trade sex for the first time. However, it is quite rare even in these situations that the young person had no prior relationship with that person. A common narrative in cases where overt force is used is that of a young cisgender woman who meets someone, typically a cisgender man close to her age, and feels as if they are building some type of relationship. At some point in their relationship building, she is forced to trade sex. The force may be physical or emotional or both. Paniz Bagheri, case manager for SAGE, described how one of her clients, a young cisgender woman, was sexually assaulted by her boyfriend and his brother, and later that same night they "took her out to the track, and they let her out of the car, and they said, 'Don't come back until you make us money.' And so that was her first . . . engagement in prostitution" (personal communication, May 3, 2012). Other cases share this theme and highlight the grooming ritual that takes place over a period of time before the young person first trades sex. A case manager in Chicago explained one such situation:

So she told me that she met her trafficker a year before. . . . [S]he was six-teen at the time, and she was walking home from somewhere, and a car approached her, and a guy was driving, the trafficker, and there was another girl who was in the car, and she was saying, "Oh, you're so cute," you know, "I want to get to know you, get in the car," you know, "Let's talk some." And then she is kind of hesitant in the beginning, but she got in, and then they told her, you know, "We're going to be your new family now," and then they eventually forced her to trade sex. (N. Yoon, personal communication, Oc-tober 31, 2011)

Although the reported percentages of young people who are overtly forced to trade sex are seemingly low, this does not mean that force is not present in the experiences of other young people. Indeed, over time, many of these young people will experience coercion, force, and violence related to trading sex. Chapter 3 explores in more detail the ways in which lives are linked and violence occurs. Here, with respect to initiation of sex trades, it is worth noting that overt force is not involved in most youth's initiation, and initiation rarely occurs overnight (Harris, Scott, and Skidmore 2006).

THE ASSOCIATION OF ABUSE WITH SEX TRADE INVOLVEMENT

A significant body of literature has positioned sexual abuse as a key factor contributing to youth involvement in sex trades (Brawn and Roe 2008; Cree 2008; Estes and Weiner 2005; Harris, Scott, and Skidmore 2006; Jes-son 1993; Kotrla 2010; Schwartz 2009; Unger et al. 1998; Weisberg 1984). Because that literature lacks comparison groups, we do not know the rates of sexual abuse among a comparable group of youth who are not involved in trading sex. In contrast, a recent study conducted in San Francisco with adult, cisgender women who use drugs found that the association between being raped as a child and current involvement in trading sex was not statistically significant. Both groups of urban poor women in that study experienced alarmingly high rates of childhood rape: 58 percent among those who trade sex and 43 percent among those who do not (Lutnick et al. 2014).

An examination of research about the association between childhood abuse and involvement in trading sex reveals inconsistent findings. In a large prospective cohort study that matched abused and neglected children with nonabused and non-neglected children, it was childhood physical abuse and neglect, not sexual abuse, that was associated with an increased risk for involvement in trading sex (Wilson and Widom 2010). As explored earlier in this chapter, when some young people are neglected by their parents or guardians, they turn to trading sex to meet their needs. Because involvement in trading sex occurs within the larger social context, it may be that other factors influence the association between childhood physical abuse and neglect and involvement in trading sex. In Helen Wilson and Cathy Widom's (2010) study, it was only when the abuse and neglect were coupled with an early sexual initiation that the association between them and trading sex remained. Likewise, Widom (1994) found that compared to nonabused and non-neglected young people, those who have experienced abuse and neglect have increased odds of running away. Once on the streets, some of these young people will turn to trading sex.

Similarly, a comparison of fifteen- to seventeen-year-olds who were and were not trading sex found that those involved in sex trades were no more likely to have been sexually abused than those with no involvement (Mc-Clanahan et al. 1999). However, research focused on young people who are homeless has found an association between abuse and trading sex. A study focused on youth who use drugs and are street involved found that both sexual and emotional abuse were independently associated with trading sex (Stoltz et al. 2007). Among young, homeless, cisgender women in Hollywood, California, those involved in sex trades reported marginally higher rates of childhood physical abuse. In that study, the entire sample experienced high rates of childhood sexual abuse, with no significant difference between those who had and had not traded sex (Warf et al. 2013).

Absent from the research literature that explores the associations between abuse and trading sex is the recognition that for some young people their involvement in sex trades is a continuation of the abuse perpetrated by their parents (Cole and Anderson 2013; Smith Vardaman, and Snow 2009). The next chapter describes how family members force their children to trade sex. It is important to note here that the parents who sexually and physically abuse their children also then force or coerce them into trading sex as a means of maintaining their domination and control. Scholar-activist Minh Dang describes how "the first survivors of trafficking I met—and they didn't identify as that, they identified as survivors of child abuse—had their mothers pimping them out and exchanging them [for] drugs and money. And so on a personal note, those close friends of mine, none of their stories are being heard or represented" (personal communication, January 16, 2014).

Although the findings about the association between abuse and involvement in trading sex are inconsistent, a common response young people have to abusive situations at home is to run away (Pierce 2012). A case manager in New York described why one of her clients stopped living at home with her grandmother and aunt: "Part of the reason why she doesn't stay there is because she says her aunt is mainly verbally and emotionally abusive, and she can't, she doesn't want to be around her, and she's always treating her terribly, so she tries to go out and find other places to live" (J. Westmacott, personal communication, March 23, 2011).

Once these young people have left the abusive situation at home, they find that they need a way to meet their survival needs for shelter, food, and money (Brittle 2008; Cobbina and Oselin 2011; Harris, Scott, and Skidmore 2006; Schwartz 2009; Warf et al. 2013). Trading sex becomes a viable option. They have decided that being at home is not the best option for them, and they are willing to do whatever it takes to avoid spending time there. Adrianna Velasquez, a case manager for STOP-IT, described the experience of a young transgender woman who had run away from home: "She obviously needed food and clothing and shelter. . . . She had to, you know, prostitute herself in order to obtain those things" (personal communication, October 31, 2011).

Some young people who have experienced sexual abuse consider trading sex to be a way to reclaim control over their bodies and sexuality and to overcome feelings of powerlessness stemming from their abuse (Cobbina and Oselin 2011; Cousart 2013; Nixon et al. 2002). A case manager in Chicago who was working with a young cisgender woman who received unwanted sexual advances from her aunt's boyfriend shared that her client said, "I don't have to put up with this. . . . [I]f I'm going to deal with this, I might as well get money for it" (E. Dalberg, personal communication, November 1, 2011). This same sentiment was expressed to Cobbina and Oselin by a cisgender woman who started trading sex as a teenager: "[In] my childhood, I had been molested. And then as time went on, I was still getting molested, so I got tired.

And I said well, if a man [is] going to take it from me, why not sell myself?" (2011, 319). In these situations, young people view trading sex as a way to meet their material and emotional needs and to regain some control over their lives.

Recent work has focused on the intersection between a history of child welfare involvement and trading sex (International Human Rights Clinic 2013; U.S. Department of Health and Human Services 2013) and has high-lighted child welfare involvement as a "major risk factor" for involvement in sex trades (Walker 2013a). Of the eighty-eight children identified as child sex-trafficking victims by the Department of Children and Families in Con-necticut, 98 percent ($n = 86$) had some type of involvement with child wel-fare services (U.S. Department of Health and Human Services 2013, 3). A report published by the California Child Welfare Council estimates that be-tween 50 and 85 percent of children who trade sex have current or former involvement with the child welfare system (Walker 2013a, 11). Speaking at the Conference to End Child Sex Trafficking in 2013, Catherine Cousart, su-pervisor for the San Francisco Human Services Agency, addressed the in-tersections between sex trades and child welfare involvement: "By nature of the children we serve, all of our children are at risk for human trafficking. Because our children are physically, sexually, emotionally abused, neglected and abandoned, they all categorically fit the definition of at-risk. . . . There's environmental deprivation due to poverty, parents' lack of resources, lack of suitable housing, lack of daily necessities, food, clothing, and violence in their neighborhoods."

A discrepancy exists "between lurid journalistic accounts and the reality" (Walkowitz 1980, 83) of most young people's involvement in trading sex. In only about 10 percent of the cases does it appear that forced engagement characterizes young people's first experiences with trading sex. At the same time, however, even when youth are not forced into trading sex, their agency is often constrained. Instead of trying to understand their initiation in isola-tion or confining it to the simplistic narrative in which a bad person forces them to trade sex, it is important to examine the structural and social con-texts in which their initiation occurs. When we do that, we see that a com-plex set of factors and crises often precedes their involvement in trading sex

(Marcus and Curtis 2013) and that socioeconomic and cultural systems have failed these young people (Marcus, Riggs, et al. 2011). Dr. Ana Mari Cauce, professor of psychology at the University of Washington, spoke about the need for a more nuanced examination of this group of young people. She recommended that we "not view these youth as all alike. We need to see them as individuals. Some have disabilities, some are LGBT, some come from the African American community, etc. The term *homeless* is just an umbrella. I think it is important to understand that they are individuals who possess amazing strengths, resiliency and are often incredibly sensitive, caring young people who have been given a bad break in life" (qtd. in Washington Coalition of Sexual Assault Programs 2004, 3).

Different routes and reasons lead this group of young people to trade sex. Common scenarios include needing to survive, wanting to fulfill emotional needs, and seeking gender and sexual identity validation. Trading sex offers young transgender women the opportunity to receive gender affirmation and to be sexually desirable. Young people who are homeless are particularly likely to trade sex as a way to meet their basic needs. Youth who are housed also turn to sex trades to meet their financial, survival, and emotional needs. In these situations, trading sex becomes a solution for youth whose families cannot or will not provide the youth's basic needs due to extreme poverty or child neglect. Gretchen Hunt, staff attorney at the Kentucky Association of Sexual Assault Programs, explains that "what unites all victims is some vulnerability. Whether it is a runaway teen who's left home because of childhood sexual abuse [or] a transgender youth who has left home because she is being ostracized . . . [t]he main unifying factor is their vulnerability" (in Shaw 2012).

It is important to address the abuse that all people may experience, but to confine the issue of young people's involvement to discussions of sexual abuse oftentimes results in ignoring the other inequalities they may face. Jes Richardson, a sex-trafficking survivor and former sex worker, reflected on what effects this intersection of childhood abuse, trafficking, and inequality had on her: "My childhood sexual abuse paved the way for me being trafficked, but it was poverty that kept me in the sex industry long after I escaped my pimp. The misconception of childhood sexual abuse being *the primary factor* in leading a person into the sex industry, excuses the need for quality economic opportunities. We must address poverty, which is unequivocally tied to racism, gender inequality, social and economic class, and a lack of community" (2014, emphasis in original).

Referring to these young people as "domestic minor victims of sex trafficking" ignores the resiliency and resourcefulness so many of them demonstrate. They are largely doing the best that they can with limited options and limited support. In essence, they are creating sexual solutions to nonsexual problems and relying on their sexual capital, which may be their greatest asset. Because they use sex to gain access to transportation, places to stay, food, clothing, and money, their involvement may actually help them make it through their adolescence alive (Schaffner 2006).

3

LINKED LIVES

THIRD PARTIES, VIOLENCE, AND TRANSITIONS IN INVOLVEMENT

No one factor in and of itself causes young people's involvement in trading sex. The dominant narrative about pimp-controlled youth results in outrage and indignation directed at these individuals instead of in a questioning of the structural factors that are the antecedents to such involvement. The lack of ambiguity in the relationships presented by the "victim industry" leads to overly simplistic ideas about young people's involvement in trading sex and positions them as one-dimensional characters who are victims (Best 1997).

The vilification of third parties is complicated by findings that many of these individuals first started off in the sex industry as people who sold sex (Birkhead 2011; Marcus, Riggs, et al. 2011; Raphael and Myers-Powell 2010). Sociologist Julia O'Connell Davidson's work highlights how "people's entry into pimping is [often] predicated upon exactly the same kind of poverty, abuse, neglect, deprivation and despair that underpins entry into prostitution" (1998, 60). In interviews with twenty-five former pimps in Chicago, Jody Raphael and Brenda Myers-Powell found that 56 percent of the cisgender men and 100 percent of the cisgender women sold sex prior to becoming pimps. They also found that 88 percent of these pimps had as children experienced physical abuse and 76 percent sexual assault (2010, 1). These findings further support the need for multidimensional portrayals of third parties involved in the experiences of young people trading sex. As a Department of Youth and Family Services worker in Atlantic City, New Jersey, offered, "Pimps are not always what we think they are" (qtd. in Marcus and Curtis 2013, 7).

Using the term *pimp* or *trafficker* limits our understanding of the dynamics involved within the relationships youths have with people who act as third parties to their involvement in sex trades. When these terms are evoked, people imagine that the young person is entirely under the control of the pimp-trafficker and that violence is a common occurrence. In addition, when the gendered and racial term *pimp* is evoked, many people picture an adult, African American, cisgender man. O'Connell Davidson describes this stereotypical characterization:

> This form of prostitution is popularly imagined to involve gullible young women whose pathetic yearning for affection and/or glamour has led them into the clutches of a male pimp who first promises them love and then proceeds to manipulate, control and brutalize them into prostitution, using extremes of violence to prevent them from exiting "the life." . . . I think there is a very real sense in which this stereotype of "the Pimp" represents a kind of folk devil constructed out of both misogynist and racist fear. Pimps are not only pictured as men who "live off" women (thereby inverting the "proper" order between the sexes) but they are also often imagined as Black males who control the sexual "fallen" women. (1998, 43)

Countering this narrow portrayal are the criminalized activities pertaining to third-party involvement in prostitution (because the list is based on criminal codes, it uses the term *prostitution*). These activities include (*a*) pimping—the act of directly or indirectly receiving earnings garnered through prostitution or asking for or receiving money in exchange for soliciting to trade sex; (*b*) pandering—the facilitation or provision of someone to be used for prostitution, including inducing, encouraging, or forcing someone to engage in prostitution; (*c*) keeping or residing in a house of prostitution; (*d*) leasing a house of prostitution; (*e*) procuring someone to travel for purposes of prostitution; (*f*) sending a minor to or permitting a minor to enter a house of prostitution; and (*g*) taking a person against his or her will for prostitution.

What this list reveals is that in addition to pimping, a diversity of activities can be conducted by third parties. Relationships with third parties can be nonexistent (in the cases where young people work independently) or extremely abusive or formal business arrangements that may or may not involve violence or friendships where young people are helping each other survive. Deanna Croce, training and outreach manager for the anti-trafficking program at Safe Horizon, has referred to the heterogeneity of experiences she encounters in her work with young people: "Sometimes we have this pimp–girl paradigm, and a lot of the stories kids told me in counseling were not that" (2014).

I have chosen to use the term *third-party involvement* to allow for the emergence of a more nuanced picture of the ways in which these young people's lives are connected with others. Throughout this text, I refer to anyone who participates in activities that fit the legal definition of pimping, pandering, or the other criminalized prostitution offenses described above as a third party. When citing research findings or directly quoting people who use other terms, such as *pimp* or *trafficker*, I leave the terms they used unchanged.

Mainstream narratives would have us believe that all young people who trade sex are controlled by a third party. Looking at the academic and social service literature, no data exists that supports this claim. Some youth service providers' accounts estimate that 50 percent of the cisgender girls they work with have a pimp (Mukasey, Daley, and Hagy 2007). Kimberly Mitchell, David Finkelhor, and Janis Wolak's analysis of arrests and detentions of minors in 2005 for crimes related to prostitution found that 57 percent of the cases were characterized as involving a third-party exploiter (2010, 24). Others' work has found that third parties are not as prevalent as we might think (Curtis et al. 2008; Marcus, Horning, et al. 2014; Williams 2010). Among 249 young people interviewed in New York City, only 8 percent of the sample reported that someone initiated their entry into trading sex (Curtis et al. 2008, 54). In that sample, 16 percent of young cisgender women, only 1 percent of young cisgender men, and none of the transgender youth reported initiation by a pimp (54). Equally revealing about the low third-party presence is that 47 percent of the New York City sample said that they did not know a single pimp (Marcus, Horning, et al. 2014, 231). Reflecting on these findings as well as on those from a study of street prostitution in Atlantic City, New Jersey, and from a study of third parties in New York City, Anthony Marcus, Amber Horning, and their colleagues comment, "Overall, our findings suggest that stereotypical pimps are far less common and important to street sex markets than would be expected, given the popular discourse and the priorities of contemporary anti-trafficking institutions" (2014, 231).

This chapter reveals how the lives of young people who trade sex are lived interdependently. A variety of people in their lives serve as third parties:

peers, friends, and acquaintances; biological and surrogate family members; and intimate partners. Some of these young people are in relationships with third parties that are best described as formal business relationships. With linked lives comes the potential for individual-level violence, however, so this chapter also describes the types of violence these young people experience in relation to trading sex. Linked lives also shape the opportunities and constraints that influence the ways in which young people move in and out of the sex industry., The chapter concludes with an examination of factors that influence these transitions.

THIRD-PARTY RELATIONSHIPS

As mentioned previously, not all young people have a third party involved in their experiences trading sex. Some research has found that self-initiation is nearly two times more common among those who start trading sex prior to the age of eighteen compared to those who start after eighteen (Marcus, Horning, et al. 2014). Studies in Atlantic City and New York City found that between 86 and 90 percent of the young people interviewed reported not having a pimp (Marcus, Riggs, et al. 2011, 9). A random sample of arrests and detentions of minors for prostitution-related crimes indicated that nearly one-third did not involve a third-party exploiter (Mitchell, Finkelhor, and Wolak 2010). Those working independently do so primarily on the street and by advertising on the Internet. Establishing a few regular clients increases youth's ability to work independently because it eliminates the need to have someone connect them to clients. A case manager in San Francisco described the experience of one young woman who worked independently: "This was really her doing her own thing; she's very self-sufficient; she kind of feels like, you know, 'Handle your business, do your business.' . . . And so she was just trying to do it on her own and . . . [to] take care of herself because her family wasn't taking care of her" (S. Larrea, personal communication, October 18, 2011).

When we look at self-reports from young people of all genders, it is more common to find that it is their peers and friends who assist with both their entry into the sex industry and their connections to clients (Curtis et al. 2008; Marcus, Horning, et al. 2014; Nixon et al. 2002; Weisberg 1984). In the study conducted by Ric Curtis and his colleagues in New York City, of the 249 young people interviewed, "girls and boys reported similar (though, surprisingly high) percentages of their 'friends' as responsible for their entry [in]to CSEC [commercial sexual exploitation of children] markets (46% and 44%, respectively), but transgender youth reported that 68% of the time, 'friends' initiated them" (2008, 46). Friends provide mentorship and guidance, and a strong ethos exists among certain groups of young people, especially those based in the street, where they look out for one another. At times, this means connecting a friend with a client, and at other times it means giving a friend some of the money they made because the friend connected them to a client (Curtis et al. 2008), all of which fit the legal definitions of pimping and pandering.

PEERS, FRIENDS, AND ACQUAINTANCES

Friends play different roles in young people's experiences trading sex. In one situation, a young cisgender woman's friend asked her if she wanted to "work for [him]," and she said yes (S. Larrea, personal communication, March 8, 2011). In another situation, a friend of a young cisgender man took him to a house where her mom, an aunt, and other adult women would give him "a lot of weed, and he has group sex with all of them" (A. Kogel-Smucker, personal communication, May 22, 2012). Among street-based youth, friends connect each other with specific clients and receive a "finder's fee" (J. Westmacott, personal communication, November 8, 2011). Other friends play a more involved role in the young person's sex trades. One young cisgender man worked out of a gay bar and paid a friend of his who was employed there to "look the other way" (J. Villarin, personal communication, March 24, 2011). Erin Knowles Wirsing, a case manager for STOP-IT, shared one young cisgender woman's description of her friend and what he did for her: "[S]he never, ever described him as her pimp. Like that, that wasn't how she viewed him. But I do know that he was helping her arrange, you know, 'dates' and getting a cut, and then he would like take her and be security outside while the sex acts were being exchanged. . . . [B]ut she never would have ever described him as a pimp. . . . He was a friend that was helping her out. . . . Not a boyfriend . . . just a friend. She had a girlfriend" (personal communication, March 2, 2011).

In other situations, friends teach each other the "tricks of the trade," such as how to find clients, avoid law enforcement, and work safely. One example is found in the story of a young cisgender woman and a friend who ran away from their group home. The young woman's case manager explained what happened after they ran out of money: "The other young woman, who was twenty years old, had . . . sex work experience, Internet based, and she told [the young woman] how to do this. . . . [T]hey both engaged in Internet-based and street-based [sex work] and made some money and were able to stay in, like, motels while they were doing this. And she reported that nobody ever forced her, and there was no violence" (J. Melendez, personal communication, May 21, 2012). In none of these examples did the young person view the third parties involved as pimps or exploiters.

In addition to youth connecting each other with clients and sharing information about how to trade sex, some young people also recruit each other to be their third party (Birkhead 2011; Busch-Armendariz, Nsonwu, and Heffron 2009). One young woman who was living in a group home was introduced by another "girl in the group home" to the guy "who allowed her to use his apartment and arranged for all the johns to come in" (E. Dalberg, personal communication, November, 1, 2011). For some young people, no clear delineation exists between the role of trading sex and the role of acting as a third party for someone else's sex trades. Particularly among street-based young people and those living in transient households, "the role of pimp and prostitute tended to be interchangeable" (Marcus, Horning, et al. 2011, 14). In these situations, the roles are interchangeable and taken on when the needs of the household members warrant them.

FAMILY: BIOLOGICAL AND SURROGATE

Youth's connections with their family members also shape their involvement trading sex. In addition to neglecting and being unable to provide for children's needs in the face of poverty, family members serve as links in other ways to their children's involvement. Some biological family members are the children's traffickers or exploiters (Cole and Anderson 2013; Croce 2014; Mitchell, Finkelhor, and Wolak 2010; Sims 2012; Smith, Vardaman, and Snow 2009). In a survey of 323 social service and juvenile justice professionals in

Kentucky, the most mentioned trafficker relationship type (at 62 percent) was a family member (Cole and Anderson 2013, 13). In their assessment of ten cities in the United States that have a human trafficking task force, Linda Smith, Samantha Vardaman, and Melissa Snow found that in each location "parents or guardians have acted as traffickers/pimps" (2009, 7). A field assessment in Las Vegas noted that approximately 30 percent of the time it was family members who were trafficking their younger relatives (Smith, Vardaman, and Snow 2009, 7). Scholar-activist Minh Dang stresses the importance of acknowledging familial involvement: "I'm going to say over and over that my parents were my pimps because people aren't hearing that. They think it's random strangers or something. I mean, come on" (personal communication, January 16, 2014). Some of the youngest ages of initiation into sex trades and the most coercion are found in parent–child pimping relationships (Marcus, Horning, et al. 2014). In part, this can be attributed to the power dynamic that exists between parents and their children. Jennifer Cole and Elizabeth Anderson explain that "when one considers parents or guardians as traffickers, the nature of the relationship between the trafficker and child has laid the foundation for the trafficker to manipulate and exploit the dependent child" (2013, 30).

In other instances, family members introduce their young relatives to the person who ultimately becomes the third party involved in the young persons' sex trades. A case manager in Chicago described what happened when one young cisgender woman went to live with her dad because her mom was going through some issues: "[T]he dad was the one that introduced her to trading sex because he linked her up with one of his friends. That's how she got introduced to the pimp [and] put out on the streets. [I]t was all because of the dad; the dad was the one that introduced this to her" (A. Velasquez, personal communication, April 25, 2012). In another situation, a young cisgender woman's sister introduced her to the person who connected her to clients and took part of the money she made from trading sex. That person was also playing the same role for the young woman's mother (E. Dalberg, personal communication, November 1, 2011). For another young cisgender woman, people her older brother brought home to stay with them ended up "pimping [her] out" (J. Westmacott, personal communication, March 25, 2011).

Some young people consider the third parties involved as surrogate family members, "like a big brother or . . . maybe a little bit of father" (N. Woodcox, personal communication, October 31, 2011). In one situation, a young cisgender woman was living with the man who coordinated her sex trades, his mother, and the other young cisgender women who were working for him. She described the mom to her case manager as "'a good church lady. She would keep people's babies if they needed to, she made hot meals, and she would be kind to us'" (qtd. in N. Woodcox, personal communication, October 31, 2011). In another situation, a young transgender woman spoke about how she viewed the third party involved in her sex trades as someone very important to her. Her case manager shared that the young woman considered this person "as more of a mother figure, as someone who really cared for her, as somebody who really understood her for who she was and praised her for wanting to live for who she wanted to be. So the trafficker pretty much gave her that attention she was not getting at home, or that attention that she really wanted. She felt someone finally understood her" (A. Velasquez, personal communication, October 31, 2011).

FORMAL BUSINESS RELATIONSHIPS

Some relationships with third parties are best viewed as formal arrangements that range from sporadic involvement to full-time management. Some youth give a percentage of their money to someone who helps them get clients. The academic literature sometimes refers to this type of third party as a "spot pimp," someone who directs clients to the young person for a small fee (typically ten dollars) but who does not have exclusive control over the young person (Marcus and Curtis 2013; Marcus, Riggs, et al. 2011). To date, however, no findings suggest that young people refer to these people as "spot pimps." Instead, they consider them to be friends and acquaintances who help them get clients and watch out for them (Marcus, Riggs, et al. 2011). These individuals typically make most of their money in other illegal-market sectors, such as drug sales, and supplement their income by connecting clients to individuals trading sex (Marcus, Horning, et al. 2014).

Full-time, formalized third-party relationships seem to be rare among young people. People who self-identify as pimps report that having young people work for them is "dangerous and unprofitable" (Marcus, Riggs, et al. 2011, 18) because they are unreliable and lack the experience and expertise to charge higher rates for their services and to attract affluent clients (Horning

2013; Marcus, Horning, et al. 2014; Marcus, Riggs, et al. 2011). This does not mean that no situations exist where young people have full-time, formalized, third-party relationships as part of their experiences trading sex. Joean Villarin, case manager for Streetwork, shared how a young cisgender woman worked out of a house where there was "an actual madam." In that situation, the young person described giving the woman "a cut of the money, and she was talking about . . . the financial workings of it all and . . . the relationships that she built with the other girls there and how they treated her" (personal communication, March 23, 2011).

INTIMATE PARTNERS

In addition to friends and acquaintances, boyfriends of young cisgender women are among the most common types of third parties. In these situations, youth do not consider their intimate partners "pimps." A case manager in Chicago explained that "whenever I use the term 'trafficker' or 'pimp,' she, you know, kind of cringes. . . . She sees her trafficker as a partner, her lover" (N. Yoon, personal communication, October 31, 2011). These third parties are in a relationship with the young person who is trading sex and sometimes are also the father of their children. Some of them directly coordinate their girlfriends' sex trades. Others, however, simply benefit from the money the young women make from trading sex. Sophia Larrea, a case manager in San Francisco, explained the relationship dynamic of one of the young cisgender women she worked with: "And she was living with [her boyfriend] sometimes as well, providing for him, so a lot of the money that she would make went to him. But she totally didn't identify him as a pimp, and I didn't get the sense that he was a pimp as well" (personal communication, October 18, 2011). Because this man benefitted financially from the young woman's trading sex, however, by law his activities constituted pimping.

Somewhat unique to young cisgender women who are street based and homeless is the theme of strategically coupling with someone who can provide shelter and protection. This "survival-focused coping" (Goodman et al. 2009, 318) results in youth making sure that they are always in a relationship with someone who has more experience navigating homelessness and being on the streets than they do. In one such case, a young cisgender woman "had broken up with [her] boyfriend, and you could see that, she came in here one day, and you could see that she was worried. . . . But then she hooked up with another guy who could offer the same things, and she was with this guy for a while and then eventually got back with the old guy. But there's never been a moment where she didn't have [a male partner], and the guy is characteristically older, bigger . . . and more homelessness history . . . and survival skills than her" (L. Davis, personal communication, May 22, 2012).

In other situations, youth form sexual relationships to secure a place to stay and thus to avoid having to sleep outside. A case manager in New York City explained how even though one of her clients was not attracted to the older man she was staying with, "he did expect her to have sex in order to stay there" (J. Westmacott, personal communication, November 8, 2011). The prospects of being alone on the street compel these young cisgender women to form relationships with men for protection.

INDIVIDUAL-LEVEL VIOLENCE

Regardless of their pathways into trading sex and whether a third party is involved or not, violence is an all too common experience for young people who trade sex. Youth's experiences trading sex are fraught with physical, emotional, and sexual violence perpetrated by clients, third parties, and the police. Among the young people receiving services from the three programs that provided intake data to me—SAGE, STOP-IT, and Streetwork—44 percent reported being physically harmed, 30 percent were threatened with harm, and 55 were coerced by promise of a future material or emotional benefit (see figure 4 in appendix E). Similar rates of physical assaults were reported by thirty-six homeless cisgender women ages eleven to twenty-three who were involved in trading sex. In that study, 38.9 percent reported being sexually assaulted; 36.1 percent being battered, beaten, or injured; and 44.4 percent being robbed (Warf et al. 2013, 1210). Many qualitative explorations of violence among this group of young people have been conducted and consequently do not provide numbers to describe the frequency of these experiences (Cobbina and Oselin 2011; Curtis et al. 2008; Gragg et al. 2007; Iman et al. 2009; Konstantopoulos et al. 2013; Marcus and Curtis 2013; Marcus, Horning, et al. 2014; Nixon et al. 2002; Raphael, Reichert, and Powers 2010;

Williams 2010). Other studies provide an overview of violence experienced but do not present any primary qualitative or quantitative data (Fong and Cardoso 2010; Grace et al. 2012; Institute of Medicine and National Research Council 2013; Kennedy and Pucci 2007; Lew 2012; Reid 2010; Smith, Vardaman, and Snow 2009; Walts et al. 2011).

Qualitative research findings are replete with themes of clients perpetrating violence against young people who trade sex (Cobbina and Oselin 2011; Iman et al. 2009). A community-based participatory empowerment project in Chicago reports that youth are physically abused, stalked, raped, and gang-raped by clients (Iman et al. 2009). A cisgender woman who started trading sex when she was fourteen reported that she "was raped many times and left for dead, having people cut my face up" (qtd. in Cobbina and Oselin 2011, 325). Paniz Bagheri relayed how one of her clients, a young cisgender woman, was kidnapped by a client and taken to a house where she was held against her will while "many men paid to have sex with her" (personal communication, October 19, 2011). Young transgender women can experience increased rates of violence because of their gender identity. Sharing one young transgender woman's experience, Johannah Westmacott, a case manager in New York City, said that "when she rejects them [men] and sometimes, you know, comes out as trans and reject[s] them, then she's been violently attacked a few times, like repeatedly, and including once with a razor blade, and she had to get stitches. And so it's just something that's kind of constant in her daily life" (personal communication, May 22, 2012). For many young transgender women, whether they are actively involved in trading sex or not, just being out on the street increases their vulnerability, and they are "harassed and propositioned by men all of the time" (J. Westmacott, personal communication, May 22, 2012). The unfortunate reality is that some youth seem to accept that violent clients are a hazard innate to trading sex.

Young people are controlled, manipulated, and abused emotionally, physically, and sexually by the third parties who are involved in their experiences trading sex. When third parties control a young person's money, they are able to manipulate the young person into doing whatever they want. Another tactic of control used by third parties is to threaten to have someone's children taken away (Iman et al. 2009). In situations when third parties are upset with a young person, they will remind them how much the youth's survival depends on them. Elyse Dalberg of the STOP-IT Program in Chicago reported the actions of a third party who was upset with a young cisgender woman because she did not bring in enough money. He "shaved her head and took her shoes in the middle of winter and threw her out on the street. A place to sleep was very based on her ability to bring money in" (personal communication, March 2, 2011). Other third parties are more emotionally and verbally than physically abusive. A case manager's description of one such person captures this dynamic: "She said he wasn't that bad all the time. . . . There were, you know, slaps and hits every now and then, but he was more so mentally abusive. He told her that she was fat and ugly a lot. [A]nd it comes across in her attitude towards herself. [S]he's like, 'Oh, I'm so ugly,' and this and that, and she's like, 'He always told me that I was ugly, and he's right.' He was more so mentally abusive to her and the other girls" (N. Woodcox, personal communication, October 31, 2011).

Even when youth are trading sex independently, they sometimes are still targeted by third parties. One young cisgender man who worked independently was told by "one of the main pimps on that . . . section of the neighborhood, 'You need to get out of my turf, or I'm going to cut your dick off and feed it to you'" (E. Knowles Wirsing, personal communication, March 2, 2011).

People who employ such physical and sexual abuse as a means of control are referred to as "gorilla pimps" by law enforcement officials (Kennedy et al. 2007), the third parties themselves (Marcus, Horning, et al. 2014), and social services providers.[1] Celia Roberts, a case manager for SAGE, explained that "a gorilla pimp is, you know, someone that's really brutal, will throw you in the trunk [of a car], will slice your face, [and] will put his markings on you" (personal communication, March 9, 2011). When young people try to leave these abusive third parties, they are assaulted in retaliation. A case manager in New York City described how when a young cisgender woman had gone to visit her abusive boyfriend, who lived in the same neighborhood as her former abusive pimp, "her pimp saw her and took her and threatened to kill her . . . and she was actually held hostage by her former pimp, who actually attempted to pimp her out for a little more than twelve hours" (J. Melendez, personal communication, May 21, 2012). It is estimated that approximately 2 percent of youth who have a pimp are coupled with these types of brutally abusive individuals and that such pimps can be the most difficult to leave, especially when they have some type of parental role, formal or informal, with respect to the young person (Marcus, Horning, et al. 2014). Speaking at the Conference to End Child Sex Trafficking, Catherine Cousart, supervisor for the San Francisco Human Services Agency, explained the reasons why some young people find it difficult to leave such relationships: "Even when the relationship progresses into domination and violence, it's often not unfamiliar and can seem like love to them. Often their self-worth is so low they don't believe they deserve much else anyway. Given their experiences, the alternating love and violent relationships can seem normal, can give the illusion of a family" (2013).

It is not uncommon to hear that young people experience violence more often from law enforcement officials than from any other group (Curtis et al. 2008; Gragg et al. 2007; Iman et al. 2009; Torres and Paz 2012). Young people on the street are easy targets for police (Bernstein and Foster 2008), and some have sustained bodily damage while being arrested when they were "out on the track" (Bagheri 2013). They "get policed a lot because they're so publically available for meeting people's [i.e., police officers'] needs [to fill] quotas and tickets" (J. Westmacott, personal communication, March 23, 2011). Young transgender women often experience significant harassment from police officers (Curtis et al. 2008; Dank 2014; Iman et al. 2009; McLemore 2013). Even when they are not trading sex, they are arrested simply because they are transgender and in a certain area—what is referred to as "walking while trans." The assumption is that because they are transgender women and walking in a certain area, they must be involved in trading sex. Case manager Nicole Woodcox said that the officers' attitude can be described as follows: "It's a bad area, we can treat the people any way we want to" (personal communication, October 31, 2011).

When asked about their experiences with police, young people report that they have been physically assaulted by them, and it is common for police officers to sexually assault them in exchange for not being arrested (Curtis et al. 2008; Gragg et al. 2007; Iman et al. 2009; Nixon et al. 2002). A young transgender woman in New Orleans reported that in 2013 "in the French Quarter [the police officer] asked what I was doing, and I said I was waiting for friends. He got out of his car and asked to see my ID and then he say I looked like a suspect and asked if I had any weapons in my purse. Then he went through my purse and found the condoms then he started asking me how much I charge for a blow job. He said if I wanted to go free I had to give him a blow job because the condoms were reason enough to bring me in so I did it and he let me go" (qtd. in McLemore 2013, 43).

This type of sexual abuse also takes place during undercover operations. Paniz Bagheri relayed the story of how during a prostitution bust a police officer sexually abused her client: "She got in his car, and he said that he didn't have money and that they were going to drive to the gas station for him to be able to use an ATM, get some gas, and get some money. And one of the things that she said was that he let her fondle him on the entire drive. She said it was at least a solid five minutes, and she, one of the things she asked me, she said, 'I don't understand. If he's an undercover cop and I'm a minor, isn't he not supposed to,' you know, 'let me do that?' . . . [T]hat's something that I do hear commonly, is that the officers seem to take definite advantage and become yet another exploiter" (personal communication, May 4, 2012). The reality is that it is common for young people who trade sex to "have been victimized by at least one police officer" (E. Dalberg, personal communication, March 2, 2011).

TRANSITIONS IN INVOLVEMENT OVER TIME

LEAVING THIRD PARTIES

The assumption that once a young person is coupled with a third party, he or she will always be coupled with that person is unfounded. Just as all relationships are dynamic and change over time, youth's relationships and involvement with third parties are also dynamic. For example, Ric Curtis and his colleagues (2008) found in New York City that over time young cisgender women report less pimp involvement. Among this New York City sample, the main reason young people provided for leaving their pimp was that they tired of not being allowed to spend the money they earned. Talking about the reasons why one young cisgender woman left her pimp, a case manager in Chicago commented that when the young woman realized that she was not getting any of the money, it was clear that the relationship wasn't "really benefitting her" (N. Woodcox, personal communication, April 25,

2012). This reasoning reflects how for some young people the longer they stay involved in trading sex, the more agency and control they have over their experiences. As they learn how to navigate the hazards of sex trades, especially those posed by clients and police, they find that they no longer need the assistance that third parties offer. In such cases, either the dynamic of the relationship becomes more equitable and the youth will stay with the person, or the young person leaves and trades sex independently (Marcus, Horning, et al. 2014).

Leaving someone who is involved as a third party depends largely on what the young person is getting out of that relationship. Marcus, Horning, and their colleagues (2014) offer insight into the dynamics of ceasing involvement with a third party. When the relationship is based on an idea of a romantic relationship, it appears that the bond is short lived. Once youth recognize that the person they thought was their intimate partner is just interested in acting like a "pimp," they leave the relationship. The ease of leaving a third party is severely compromised, however, when the relationship is coercive, abusive, and violent, including those instances when the people acting as a third party are formal or informal parents. In these types of relationships, they will utilize emotional, social, physical, and sexual abuse as well as the youths' economic dependence on them as means of maintaining the relationship. When young people try to leave these types of parent–child relationships, they are at great risk. One account of a young cisgender woman in New York provides an example of this type of abuse in response to the young woman's attempt to leave the relationship: "He saw me with my friend and he told me to get in the car or he'll kill me in front of my friend. So I got in the car and he took me to his house. . . . I told him that I had to see my probation officer in the morning, and he said, 'No, you're not going nowhere.' So that night, he forced me to have sex with him" (qtd. in Marcus, Horning, et al. 2014, 236)

The dynamics of these relationships are comparable to the dynamics of other types of abusive relationships. According to activist and writer Emi Koyama, "Pimping relationships that are abusive can be understood in the same way: while some people are forced to trade sex because of the violence, many remain in the pimping relationship for the same reason many abuse victims stay with their abusers: they get something out of the relationship they are not getting elsewhere" (2011a, 14).

DISENGAGING FROM TRADING SEX

Among the clients profiled in my interviews with case managers in Chicago, New York City, and San Francisco, approximately 75 percent were not currently trading sex. Young people transition in and out of trading sex with some regularity. Just as we need to examine the ways in which lives are interconnected to understand initiation of sex trades, such interconnections also need to be considered when thinking about how young people stop trading sex. Some young people stop trading sex when they decide it is not "healthy for them," "not fun anymore," or something that was just part of "a time in my life, [and] I'm going to get past it" (N. Woodcox, personal communication, April 24, 2012). These young people disconnect from peers they had been involved with, and some leave town to "get away from temptation" (E. Dalberg, personal communication, April 24, 2012).

Other youth transition away from trading sex when they experience some type of crisis. One young cisgender woman realized after being arrested and put on probation that if she started trading sex again, she would jeopardize her chance to get off of probation and become self-sufficient once she turned eighteen. Others realize that they are experiencing and witnessing increased amounts of violence out on the street, so they stop. Sometimes this decision is preceded by "a couple of bad experiences out there" (S. Larrea, personal communication, October 18, 2011). For example, one young cisgender woman decided she wanted to stop after her "pimp and his friends gang-raped her" for being away and not coming back with money (P. Bagheri, personal communication, May 3, 2012). Other young people stop trading sex after long periods of incarceration or hospitalization. Elyse Dalberg explained how one of her clients, a young cisgender woman, momentarily stopped trading sex when "she ended up hospitalized again. She'd been dragged down the street by a john, . . . got a staph infection . . . was hospitalized . . . [and was] actually unable to go back out onto the streets, which was a really good thing" (personal communication, November 1, 2011). Young people stop trading sex when the reasons why they started are addressed through other means. In their interviews with youth in New York City, Curtis and his colleagues found that 87 percent reported wanting to stop trading sex, but for more than half of them their economic and housing insecurities prevented them from doing so (2008, 102). Echoing this finding, Meredith Dank, senior researcher at the Urban Justice Institute, reports that in her interviews with young people who trade sex, "some of the main reasons youth give for not being able to stop trading is [sic] basic needs not being met. So the need for shelter, food, counseling, those types of things, job opportunities[,] got mentioned a lot" (2014).

When other people are able to meet the youth's needs, the youth don't trade sex. In some situations, this happens when family members become more involved in the youth's lives and provide for their basic needs and desires. One young cisgender woman was able to stop when she started to live with her grandmother, who was "able to spend more one-on-one time with her; give her the attention that she needs. Grandma has told her if she does well in school [and doesn't] run away, she will get her hair done, things that she wants. . . . And so [she] is starting to realize, like, 'I don't need to go out to get the things that I want'" (N. Woodcox, personal communication, April 25, 2012).

In other situations, even though family members are not physically present to attend to their children's needs, they leave them with enough money that they can survive on their own. Sometimes the resources that young people receive from social service providers allow them not to have to trade sex. Johannah Westmacott explained one such situation: "[Trading sex is] more about, like, meeting his needs. So when he needs something, he knows he can do that, and since he's had other ways to meet his needs, you know, through this program we've bought him some clothes and shoes when he needed it, and he can come here and get food, and we got him an unlimited [public transportation] card one time. . . . And so because of those kind of things and kind of meeting basic survival needs . . . he doesn't need to [trade sex] anymore" (personal communication, March 23, 2011).

REENGAGING TRADING SEX

After periods of not trading sex, young people typically reengage when they have no other way to meet their basic needs. It is clear from the examples given in the preceding section that youth will experience the same vulnerabilities of involvement if and when family members or social service providers are no longer willing or able to support them. Elyse Dalberg talked about the ways in which parental neglect resulted in one of her clients needing to reengage in trading sex. She "was forced to prostitute because she didn't have diapers for her son. [H]er mom wasn't buying her food, and her mom wasn't buying her clothes, and so she felt like that was her only option for survival" (personal communication, March 2, 2011). In some situations, when people the young person rely on to provide for them (i.e., parents, guardians, or intimate partners) either leave or are incarcerated, going back to trading sex becomes inevitable because the young person has no other means by which to support himself or herself.

For young people who are trading sex to meet their survival needs, it is difficult to think about transitioning away from or stopping their involvement in trading sex because that involvement has always been on an as needed basis (J. Westmacott, personal communication, March 23, 2011). Some of these youth "have no interest in continuing to engage in sex work, but the reality of not having a lot of resources and needing money" is enough for them to trade sex again (P. Bagheri, personal communication, May 25, 2012). For other young people, when their families struggle financially, the "fast cash" that trading sex can offer is very tempting.

The emotional attachment some young people have with people who act as third parties and their attachment to other youth involved in sex trades also pull them back into trading sex. After being back at home for a while, some youth leave again to reunite with their intimate partners, who are also the ones coordinating their sex trades. A case manager described how for one young cisgender woman it was the support provided by other youth who were working with her pimp that pulled her back into that life: "She also has a lot of friends who are connected to the life, and so when you have a support system, when you develop that support system, it's a lot easier to be engaged in it, if that's where all your friends are. So she had cut that off for a while when we were working together. But when things get hard, you go to people you can trust, and things got hard [for her]" (E. Dalberg, personal communication, November 1, 2011). Youth whose support system comprises people who trade sex turn to that support system when things become difficult. One cisgender young woman's "sister was actively engaged [in trading sex], and she always maintained contact with her sister. And so when that's always an option, that's going to be her fallback" (E. Dalberg, personal communication, November 1, 2011).

Among young people who were initially drawn to the excitement of trading sex, it can be difficult for them to completely stop their involvement. A case manager in San Francisco described how "it's exciting" for one cisgender young woman, "and she gets pulled in" (P. Bagheri, personal communication, October 18, 2011). After periods of not trading sex, some young people get bored and decide, "I'm going to go back out there and have fun" (S. Larrea, personal communication, March 8, 2011). For others, it is the combination of the desire for excitement and a need for money. "On a whim," one cisgender young woman decided to go away for the weekend with her boyfriend. When they ran out of money and had no way to get home, she "posted an ad on the Internet" (S. Larrea, personal communication, October 18, 2011).

Regardless of the reason why these young people reengage in trading sex, the reality is that many of them know that trading sex is "something [they] could always go back to" (J. Westmacott, personal communication, May 22, 2012). Minh Dang, reflecting on this absence of a youth-centered focus in our culture, explains:

So I think around child sex trafficking if we really focus on building healthy, emotional children and what's needed for that, all the systems needed to make that happen, if we address that, then my eleven-year-old niece, if shit hit the fan for her, she's not going to think, "I need to go sell myself." She's going to think, "I have these adults who are in my corner, and they'll help figure something out." And she's not living in a neighborhood where she has violence walking down the street, where she's going to be solicited and pressured. She's not going to a school where she is hated because she's black; she's at a school that values her. So she's in [a] micro-, meso-, macro-space that facilitates her holistic development. So I don't think we are really child centered in our society at all. (personal communication, January 16, 2014)

A more nuanced understanding of the types of relationships young people have with third parties makes clear how youth involvement in trading sex is not a simple story of victims and villains. We instead face the complexities of the young people themselves and the multiplicity of their experiences and relationships connected to trading sex. Some youth are being forced to trade sex by parents, family members, and intimate partners. Some youth on the street are trying to help each other with their survival needs. Others are seeking emotional support and validation. At times, they get this support and validation from their peers, clients, and people who manage their sex trades. Some of these relationships are healthy; others are abusive.

If our national and state policies were more strongly focused on meeting young people's self-identified needs instead of on trying to catch the "bad guys" and prosecute them, we likely would have a better chance of being of service to these youth. None of the federal or local responses adequately attend to the root factors that are associated with young people trading sex. When young people have other ways of meeting their needs, most will not trade sex. Our focus should therefore be attuned to the ways in which our social and cultural systems have failed these young people

4

SERVICE NEEDS AND MICROSYSTEM CHALLENGES

Young people who trade sex have a variety of needs. For instance, they will present with reproductive and sexual health needs (Decker et al. 2012; Konstantopoulos et al. 2013; Nixon et al. 2002), including birth control and abortion services, routine sexual health screenings, treatment for sexually transmitted infections, and ongoing care for conditions such as HIV. For young people who use drugs, some will want access to harm reduction services such as needle exchange, and some will want to enroll in substance use treatment programs (U.S. Senate 2005). Because of the pervasive, everyday violence some of these young people experience, many will have the same physical and mental health needs as others who have been physically, sexually, or emotionally assaulted (Clawson and Grace 2007; Gragg et al., 2007; U.S. Senate 2005).

Many service providers cite mental health care as these young people's greatest need. A survey of social service providers in Kentucky found that seven out of ten professionals who work with youth who trade sex made this claim (Cole and Anderson 2013, 17). In this same survey, three out of ten reported that basic needs such as housing and financial assistance were the greatest needs (17). However, when youth are asked what their most pressing needs are, they most often cite employment and housing (Curtis et al. 2008). These young people's immediate priority is making sure their basic survival needs for shelter, food, clothing, and financial support are met.

The monthly data provided to me by the three programs about their clients' needs make clear that young people who trade sex have multiple needs (see table 4.1). These needs range from crisis planning to support with education and employment goals, and accessing benefits and health care.

TABLE 4.1 CLIENT-IDENTIFIED SERVICE NEEDS

SERVICE	NUMBER OF TIMES REQUESTED*	PERCENTAGE OF TIMES RECEIVED
Support/crisis intervention	298	97
Education	263	63
Mental health	250	68
Food/clothing	231	94
Safety planning	214	90
Employment	165	46
Sexual health	154	78
Family reunification/counseling	154	57
Assistance with benefits	118	55
Victim assistance/legal advocacy	117	83
Long-term housing	112	27
Medical assistance	105	90
Emergency housing	102	46
Transportation	98	99
Substance/alcohol abuse	81	58
Transitional housing	62	29
Hygiene services and supplies	47	100
Dental services	26	42
Social services advocate	16	100
Legal forms of identification	13	54
Life skills	12	100
Safer injection equipment	12	100
Child care	7	57

* A SERVICE COULD BE REQUESTED MULTIPLE TIMES.

SOURCE: COMPILED FROM MONTHLY DATA PROVIDED TO THE AUTHOR BY SAGE, STOP-IT, AND STREETWORK

It is not surprising that programs are most able to meet needs when they can be provided in house or with widely available resources. Of the needed services that were received by youth at least 90 percent of the time, all are services that the programs offer in house. Needed services received between 60 and 89 percent of the time are those primarily provided elsewhere but widely available. The service needs least likely to be met—housing, employment, and dental services—reflect gaps in available services and the challenges of connecting young people to services that require planning.

Similar to the way in which life course theory (Elder 1998) positions people within structural, social, and cultural contexts to better understand their actions, Urie Bronfenbrenner's (1979) ecological systems theory also relies on a person-in-the-environment approach. Microsystems are social settings in which direct face-to-face contact takes place, such as that between case managers and their clients. The rest of this chapter describes the microsystem challenges that case managers and other program staff experience in their work with young people who trade sex. Some young people are simply disinterested in accessing social services (Marcus and Curtis 2013), and others feel that being on the streets is "less harmful and more likely to help them survive than the programs offered in the community" (Williams 2010, 252). Once young people are connected with services, other challenges arise that are owing to common teenage attributes such as expecting things to happen immediately and engaging only sporadically. As young people age, they developmentally become more ready to be independent. This developmental reality is in conflict, however, with the ways in which their options for independence are limited until they turn eighteen. As a consequence, case managers and program staff face the challenge of working with young people who are waiting until they reach the age of majority and have more options. Other challenges reflect the ways in which factors relating to social desirability cloud the interactions between young people and program staff. Still others are attributable to the inner workings of the agencies themselves. Program eligibility requirements and staff turnover can introduce specific challenges at the microsystem level.

SENSE OF IMMEDIACY

When young people want to meet with a specific case manager or receive a certain service, but that person of service is not immediately available, it is not uncommon for them to leave a program. The requirement that advance arrangements be made for services is largely not compatible with a sense of immediacy. Case managers shared how for many of their clients planning ahead is difficult. Nara Yoon, a case manager in Chicago, reflected that one young cisgender woman "tends to wait until the last minute to tell me what she needs. . . . She just says, 'There's no food in our refrigerator'; she has, like, nothing to eat; then in my mind, 'She should have told me like a week ago or something,' so I could request cash and then meet with her and maybe even go shopping with her" (personal communication, April 24, 2012).

Even in instances when ample time exists to plan ahead and go through the necessary steps, some young people become disenchanted with lengthy, bureaucratic processes and forego accessing what they need. Joean Villarin, a case manager in New York, explained how this disenchantment played out for one young person she worked with: "[T]here were a few times where he seemed like really interested in getting his own benefits . . . he has no identification, and we could try to work on getting ID. . . . So oftentimes he'd be like, 'Well, can I just get a letter that says I come here, so I can take this to the public assistance office?'" (J. Villarin, personal communication, March 24, 2011). In this case, the young cisgender man decided he did not want to have to go through all the necessary steps to obtain his own benefits and instead would wait until he turned eighteen, when the paperwork would, he hoped, become less burdensome.

"WAITING TO BE EIGHTEEN"

"Waiting to be eighteen" is a pervasive reality for these young people. They desperately want to be independent, and they do not want service providers telling them what to do. Elyse Dalberg in Chicago described the perspective of one young cisgender woman who was in the child welfare system: "She was really struggling with being involved in the system and not being able to decide what she wants to do for herself, feeling like because she's involved in [child welfare], they're dictating every move that she makes, and in her mind she's had to fend for herself since she was really young, and so [she has a] 'Why do I have to listen to you when I can do this on my own?' type of attitude" (personal communication, April 24, 2012).

For other young people, this desire for independence results in their being reticent to receive support from the programs because they feel they should be able to take care of themselves. Their age, though, limits their options for independence. However, many believe that once they turn eighteen, better and more housing and employment options will be available. For example, one young cisgender man was looking for housing. His case manager talked to him about his options and what type of advocacy she could undertake on his behalf. He did not want any of the options and decided, "Well, I'm just going to wait until I turn eighteen" (J. Villarin, personal communication, March 24, 2011). Some of these young people feel as if nothing in their lives can change until they are eighteen. They are therefore ambivalent about the (limited) options that are currently available to them, which makes it difficult for case managers to be of assistance to them.

SPORADIC PROGRAM ENGAGEMENT

Sporadic program engagement also poses challenges for case managers (Bernstein and Foster 2008). Young people's inconsistent program involvement inhibits case managers' ability to communicate important next steps toward accessing requested services and resources. Likewise, it is not uncommon for youth to miss scheduled appointments or to decide that they do not want the service after all. Some clients' ambivalence and lack of follow through may be attributable to their current situation. Although some may be able to identify what they need, they may not be ready to access those services. For others, sporadic engagement and lack of follow-through may reflect the presence of competing priorities.

Young people who trade sex have multiple responsibilities in their lives. Because of these competing priorities, making it to specific appointments or taking the next step toward an identified goal may not always be at the top of their list of things they feel they should do. This is particularly true for young people who are homeless and who need to prioritize their survival needs (Bernstein and Foster 2008). Sometimes it is the rigidity of programs and their heightened expectations that result in the lack of follow-through or in exit altogether from programs. At the annual Freedom Network Conference, Magalie Lerman, codirector of Prax(us), spoke about the impact of unrealistic expectations: "I definitely think that anyone in this field should work their own program. I think it's really hard to have a twenty-hour-a-week program, and then go to three trauma groups a week, and then have a personal therapist and all of those things. Sometimes people feel like they are just set up to fail and they just leave because it is too much for them at that time" (2014).

Other responsibilities such as providing care for their own children or siblings can also prevent young people from being able to access services. For those who are still attending school, trying to schedule appointments around school also proves to be challenging. For example, a young cisgender man wanted to schedule a shopping trip with his case manager. Because he was in school, however, he could go only after school, but that was the time the case manager had to be available onsite for other clients (A. Kogel-Smucker, personal communication, May 22, 2012).

TRUST ISSUES

Regardless of involvement in trading sex, young people of all genders, races, and ethnicities are frequently slow to trust service providers (Farrow et al. 1992; Fine et al. 2003). This is true for homeless youth (Barry, Ensign, and Lippek 2002; Bernstein and Foster 2008; Kurtz et al. 2000; Moore 2005; Pollio et al. 2006); for youth in urban, rural, and tribal areas (Fine et al. 2003; Garringer 2005); for transitional youth ages eighteen to twenty-four with and without severe emotional disturbance (County of San Diego Behavioral Health Services 2011; Davis 2003); and for youth chronically exposed to violence and poverty (Greene 1993). Knowing that young people who trade sex are also part of these larger communities, we should not be surprised that program staff and case managers report the challenge of establishing trust with their clients.

The early experiences of some of these young people may inhibit their ability to trust others. A common response to being exploited or victimized by adults is to be distrustful of adults in general, including those in service agencies and positions of authority (Farrow et al. 1992). Some of these young people have "fled child welfare or juvenile justice institutions (such as group homes) they found coercive or stigmatizing, and so are particularly unlikely to trust providers they feel are imposing rigid demands or 'telling them what their problem is'" (Bernstein and Foster 2008, 102). When prior experiences with social services agencies have not met their needs, young people will either avoid future social service engagement or will be appropriately suspicious of service providers (Moore 2005). In interviews with young adults who stayed in shelters, group homes, or alternative home placements before they reached the age of eighteen, P. David Kurtz and his colleagues learned that "breaking confidentiality, pathologizing youth, not keeping promises, and [treating youth] like an object" are the types of behaviors that contribute to young people's distrust of social service providers (2000, 394). As young people age, they often have numerous experiences with "helping agents" that result in "significant mistrust" (Davis 2003, 500). Paniz Bagheri, a case manager in San Francisco, offered the following thought about trust at the San Francisco Collaborative Against Human Trafficking 2013 Conference to End Child Sex Trafficking: "Most of all we need to meet clients where they're at and build trust. . . . Each individual has their own story, has their own identity, and often times that has not been treasured or valued" (2013).

Somewhat unique to young people who trade sex are the ways in which the criminalization of prostitution and other status offenses affect their ability to trust case managers and other program staff. This theme is explored further in chapter 7, which examines the macrosystem challenges. It is worth noting here that "being picked up by the police only increases [youth's] distrust of everyone who is an authority figure, including child social service providers" (Reid 2013).

SOCIAL DESIRABILITY

Most young people in the social service system, including those involved in trading sex, are good at telling case managers what they think they want to hear (Banovic and Bjelajac 2012). For example, it is rare for youth to request mental health services, largely because they do not think they are "crazy" (N. Woodcox, personal communication, October 31, 2011). However, when case managers explore the idea of seeing a therapist, some clients will "say yes because that's supposedly what we want to hear, but when we're ready to initiate that process," the clients are not interested in receiving the service (A. Velasquez, personal communication, April 25, 2012). Case managers' prioritization of mental health services can be witnessed in the quantitative data about services requested. Table 4.1 shows that this service was requested frequently. However, interviews with case managers revealed how the youth they work with are largely disinterested in receiving mental health services. Thus, we can surmise that although case managers reported that the client identified needed mental health service, in fact it was the case manager who felt the service was needed.

Youth's inclination toward doing what is considered socially desirable is not surprising given that these young people have had "a lot of experience . . . of other people telling [them] about [their] lives and telling [them] what's going on and defining [their] relationships and being in [their] business" (J. Westmacott, personal communication, November 8, 2011). Young people may also disengage from services when they feel as if their actions are in conflict with what they think the case manager wants for them. Programs that are explicit with their clients about how they want to see them stop trading sex run the risk of alienating youth from services when they continue their involvement. The impact of such a judgmental approach to this work is described in the following example given by a case manager about her work with a young cisgender woman: "I think that the reason she hasn't talked to me lately is, it's kind of like when I was a teenager, you know. I knew what standard my mom had for me, and if I knew that I wasn't living up to that standard, I didn't really want to face her about it, right? I think that that's where we are right now . . . she respects me and values our relationship enough that she doesn't want to disappoint me in her eyes, and so I think that's where her pullback has happened . . . she knows that she's kind of reverting back to something that, for lack of a better phrase, I don't approve of" (E. Dalberg, personal communication, November 1, 2011).

Fiona Mason, supervising social worker for Safe Horizon's Anti-trafficking Program, highlights the limitations of approaching case management in such a parental, judgmental way: "What is not helpful in providing services to youth is to be parental, come from a stance of knowing what's best, and to be disingenuous and above all to be judgmental in tone and appearance. Youth can smell judgment even without someone saying a word through nonverbal communication. This can be done by well-meaning staff who may feel they are nonjudgmental but may display or communicate a judgmental approach that will not only be counterproductive, will prevent open communication and trust to be established. Without establishing a trusting relationship with the youth, very little in-depth and meaningful work can be achieved" (2013).

PROGRAM ELIGIBILITY REQUIREMENTS

If programs base service eligibility on the disclosure of involvement in trading sex, the understandably guarded nature from this group of youth proves challenging. Young people who trade sex rarely come forward and say that they are domestic minor victims of sex trafficking (Reid 2010). Marissa Castellanos, project manager for Kentucky Rescue & Restore, acknowledges that "none of the victims that I've served have self-identified" (in Shaw 2010). Katherine Chon, senior adviser in trafficking in persons at the U.S. Department of Health and Human Services, similarly reflected that "victims don't necessarily raise their hands and identify as victims" (2013). Absent referrals from law enforcement, programs do not know a priori if a youth is trading sex. For these types of programs, this means that some young people will never disclose that they trade sex and consequently will be precluded from accessing certain services. Program staff at Streetwork described how some youth will share just enough information so they can be enrolled in the trafficking program funded by the Office for Victims of Crime. For example, one young cisgender woman was very guarded about whether she was trading sex, but once she realized she could get additional resources, she was willing to acknowledge it. After that, however, she never talked about any of the specifics related to her involvement (J. Westmacott, personal communication, March 25, 2011). It is not uncommon to hear that young people do not want to disclose these specifics or that it takes months before they are willing to share some information about their experiences. Fiona Mason suggests that to foster an environment where youth feel safe opening up, a program "should not [push youth] to disclose more than they are comfortable or to disclose information before they are comfortable. When youth can control who knows what information about them, and they see that others are respecting their boundaries and following confidentiality policies, they generally learn that a worker or program is trustworthy and at that point they may feel safe to share more information" (2013).

STAFF TURNOVER

Once a young person forms a relationship with a case manager and has begun to trust that person, challenges still exist. Staff turnover in community-based organizations is the norm (Soloman 1986). Some case managers consider their work with young people who trade sex to be "more overwhelming and difficult to deal with emotionally than [work with] other vulnerable populations" (Kliner and Stroud 2012) and believe that this greater difficulty is one of the contributing factors to staff turnover in programs for this population. Some case managers I spoke with similarly voiced their concerns about the lack of or inadequate training and support they receive from their organizations. Although it is considered a best practice to maintain a consistent case-management team (Stewart 2013), many agencies are not able to offer their case managers a salary that reflects the job's high demands (Clawson and Dutch 2008; Glisson and Durick 1988; Illback and Neil 1995). In their evaluation of children, youth, and families mental health systems, Robert Illback and T. Kerby Neill found that service providers are often "poorly remunerated (in relation to other program professionals), overworked, unappreciated, and, in general, devalued" and that "such conditions inevitably give rise to high turnover rates and ineffective functioning, despite service coordinators' typical youth and enthusiasm" (1995, 24).

In situations where a client connects with a program staff member and that person leaves the organization or transfers to a different position, some young people will disengage with the program. For example, one young person "for a while avoided [the program], and when I was checking in with her she said that she, I mean, she didn't want to meet a new case manager, she wasn't interested in that. You know, she seemed to have some resentment about [her case manager] changing positions and being assigned to someone else" (J. Villarin, personal communication, May 22, 2012). In this particular situation, the case manager shared that this young cisgender woman had experienced a lot of rejection in her life. Her case manager changing positions played into this narrative, and the young person interpreted it as yet another experience in which someone she cared about left her.

To address some of the microsystem challenges discussed in this chapter, programs need to truly meet young people where they are at. Paniz Bagheri, case manager at SAGE, explains that "the work is long term, the work is not linear, there's no real roadmap to follow, there's no quick answer, no formula to plug in" (2013). The reality is that most of these young people are "not the ones coming in saying I'm being trafficked . . . they're the ones coming in mouthing off to the registration person. They're mad, they're angry, they've been up for three nights" (Chaffee 2013). But their anger is an adaptive and understandable reaction to the systems with which they interact (Croce 2014).

Establishing trust with young people is imperative. In his piece about effectively working with young people who have experienced violence and poverty, Michael Greene comments that "we cannot expect them to come rushing to our thoughtfully designed programs unless they can be convinced that 'our' place is OK" (1993, 111–112). Arlene Schneir and her colleagues (2007) offer suggestions for how best to establish relationships of trust between young people and service providers. Programs that offer assistance with "no strings attached" and low-threshold services such as showers, meals, and a place to hang out are best suited to allowing trust to develop over time. They also recommend ensuring that young people's immediate needs are met. Doing so addresses the reality that many of these young people have had their needs disregarded or dismissed by other providers (Bernstein and Foster 2008; Davis 2003; Kurtz et al. 2000; Moore 2005). Young people vote with their feet. If they are not coming to a program or stop attending once they are no longer mandated to attend, it means the program is not meeting their needs.

Programs that utilize a strengths-based model, wherein youth are empowered and recognized as the experts, are necessarily better equipped to meet these particular young people's needs. When programs and services are created as things that are done to young people as opposed to developed in partnership with them, it is not surprising that these efforts are met with resistance (Anderson 2000; Frensch and Cameron 2002; Ungar 2005b). Maryann Davis suggests that

the most pressing need is for young people to provide a guiding voice in the development of policies and services designed to serve them. The system implicitly communicates a developmentally inappropriate message when young people are left out of the equation. Young people cannot be expected to take responsibility for themselves when systems communicate that they are not capable of making decisions about their own treatment or services. Most importantly, no one knows better than the young people themselves what appeals to them. Policies, practices, and treatments without their voices are likely to fail. (2003, 505)

Reverend Alika Galloway, who works at Kwanzaa's Northside Women's Center with cisgender women who trade sex, notes that when people are allowed to "define success for themselves . . . [t]his is true empowerment" (qtd. in Lew 2012, 16). When young people identify their needs and the types of services that will best address those needs, when their input about service delivery is continuously sought, and when their suggestions about changes to program operation are incorporated, they are more likely to trust service providers (Barry, Ensign, and Lippek 2002). Inverting the hierarchical nature of service provision allows young people to direct how resources should be developed and offered (Anderson 2000; Ungar 2005b).

5

MESOSYSTEM CHALLENGES

INTERACTIONS BETWEEN CASE MANAGERS AND OTHER SYSTEMS

The multiple service needs of young people who trade sex make it unlikely that one system will be able to address their needs adequately. In isolation, systems such as child welfare and juvenile/criminal justice are not meeting these needs (Institute of Medicine and National Research Council 2013). A system of care where necessary services are coordinated across agencies is better suited to "meet the multiple and changing needs" of these youth (Stroul and Friedman 1986, 3). It is therefore critical to have a functioning system of service coordination and interagency collaboration (Manteuffel, Stephens, and Santiago 2002). Although the need for a system of care is well established, the historic fragmentation of interagency service delivery between child welfare, mental health, and juvenile justice is thoroughly documented (Burns and Friedman 1990; Dougherty et al. 1987; Duchnowski and Friedman 1990; Glisson and Hemmelgarn 1998; Rivard and Morrissey 2003; Stroul et al. 2002; Ungar 2005a; Wharf 2002; Zlotnick and Marks 2002). This fragmentation poses extensive mesosystem challenges for program staff.

This chapter explores the challenges in interagency interaction. Because young people who trade sex are represented in the child welfare and juvenile justice systems, it examines the challenges of interfacing with those two systems. For young people who are not involved in these systems, working with their parents or legal guardians also poses unique challenges. Regardless of the system or individual, issues of "turf," the absence of services, and competing priorities strain interagency collaboration.

CHILD WELFARE SYSTEM

My interviews with program staff highlight what others have found: "already overburdened," the child welfare system is particularly challenging to work with (Clawson Dutch 2008, 4). In an exploratory study of child welfare caseworkers' descriptions of their work, Brenda Smith and Stella Donovan found that their everyday practices "fall short of the family-centered, strengths-based practices promoted in casework training" (2003, 542). The report *Building a Child Welfare Response to Child Trafficking* (Walts et al. 2011) highlights how the child welfare system lacks the institutional capacity to address the issue of young people who trade sex. In its guidance to states and services, the Administration for Children, Youth, and Families of the U.S. Department of Health and Human Services has "strongly encouraged" child welfare agencies "to build internal capacity in working specifically with victims of human trafficking." (U.S. Department of Health and Human Services 2013, 13).[1]

Many young people who trade sex have been involved with the child welfare system, and it has not met their needs (Brittle 2008). The involvement in sex trades of yet others within the system is never identified (Fong and Cardoso 2010). The problem in both cases is that "many state child welfare agencies fail to see child victims of trafficking as part of their mandate" (Walts et al. 2011, 113). Katherine Walts and her colleagues also highlight that the failure to identify and serve young people who trade sex may happen because child welfare professionals lack knowledge and training about these young people. Through pre- and post-training surveys, they found that child welfare staff "consistently did not self-identify as having knowledge about legal protections, public benefits, non-governmental organizations, and special programs designated for child victims of trafficking" (2011, 103).

Case managers and program staff talk about the challenges that occur when some child welfare workers do not follow up and investigate reports. This happens in particular with older youth, whom child welfare staff "[don't] really go out of their way to investigate" (J. Westmacott, personal communication, March 23, 2011) in hopes that they can just wait for the youth to turn eighteen and then "not have to be responsible for [them] at all" (J. Melendez, personal communication, May 21, 2012). Some child welfare caseworkers may not follow up on reports about older youth because they feel pressured by the high number of children who are part of their system and because "there's this real push to get these kids off the state's budget" (Smith and Donovan 2003, 546). When a hierarchical structure encourages workers to try to minimize the number of youth provided for by the state, it is not surprising to hear that reports about older youth are not investigated.

In other situations, some child welfare caseworkers do not maintain communication with case managers at community-based organizations, so that as a result case managers do not know what is happening with their clients. Jackie Melendez from Streetwork in New York explained one such situation: "And her social worker, her assigned social worker at [child welfare], was not returning calls. There are documented notes, note after note after note, 'Ms. So-and-So does not return call,' 'Ms. So-and-So does not return call,' for like weeks" (personal communication, May 21, 2012). Because frontline child welfare workers are faced with time limitations, they deprioritize tasks they do not consider to be most important (Lin 2000). If the task does not include "child visits, court appearances, and case documentation," it is "[p]erceived as outside the realm of a caseworker's core activities" (Smith and Donovan 2003, 549). Therefore, it is possible that child welfare workers also deprioritize communication with other case managers.

The inaccessibility of some child welfare workers proves particularly troubling for those young people who are wards of the state. In one particular instance, a young person in Chicago wanted to be linked to mental health services, but her case manager was faced with the challenge of getting her child welfare worker to sign the consent forms that would allow her access to therapy: "[B]ecause she is a ward of the state, I can't put her into therapy; her [child welfare] caseworker has to sign her into therapy . . . because they're her guardian. . . . [The caseworker has to] come over here physically and sign all the paperwork. . . . Because [child welfare] caseworkers usually have a load of like sixty to a hundred kids, and they're not all in [the city] . . . she can't get here on a day that's appropriate for the counselor and that's good for the client" (N. Woodcox, personal communication, March 1, 2011). Because the child welfare caseworker was challenged by a caseload that was both large and geographically dispersed, and because the youth required that caseworker's signature to commence therapy, the young person was not able to receive the mental health care she requested.

In their work with clients involved in child welfare, case managers are often in a difficult position. Child welfare caseworkers are overextended and unavailable, and yet situations occur where they reprimand case managers for being too involved in a young person's life. Elyse Dalberg, a case manager in Chicago, expanded on this theme: "I think they were uncomfortable with how much she was trusting me, because she would come to me when she needed support because she knew that I was there and she knew that I understood her circumstances and did not feel at all supported by the staff at the home" (personal communication, March 2, 2011).

Some case managers report being told by caseworkers at group homes that they should "completely pull out" of their clients' cases and lives (E. Dalberg, personal communication, November 1, 2011) or being reprimanded because they are "too involved" (E. Dalberg, personal communication, March 2, 2011). Child welfare caseworkers may feel threatened that their clients open up to case managers about things they would never talk to the caseworkers about, so they may attempt to get the case managers out of the picture (E. Dalberg, personal communication, November 1, 2011).

Case managers I interviewed described egregious harms their clients experience because of child welfare involvement. Situations where young people are "tricked into signing themselves out of care and signing themselves out of benefits" require specific advocacy by case managers (M. Benedetto, personal communication, November 8, 2011). This advocacy often focuses on helping the young person navigate the child welfare system in order to sign himself or herself back into care. As one case manager reflected, "The level of fraud that [child welfare] commits against clients and just outright lying, it's ludicrous" (J. Westmacott, personal communication, May 21, 2012). As part of a participatory-action research project, young people in Chicago shared multiple stories about harms experienced through the foster care system (Iman et al. 2009). They recounted how "foster care settings would deny girls privileges like bus fare or clothing," forcing the girls to figure out "ways to replace those items" (Iman et al. 2009, 36). Young people also report being propositioned by and verbally abused by group home staff (Nixon et al. 2002). Shalita O'Neale, executive director of the Maryland Foster Youth Resource Center, explained, "A lot of people feel that once [youth] are ... placed into foster care that it's a better situation for them, that they're safe now and that everything is okay. And that may be the case for a lot of foster youth, but for many that isn't the case. ... There's a lot of sexual, physical, and emotional abuse within foster care itself" (qtd. in Institute of Medicine and National

Research Council 2013, 100). When youth experience this type of structural violence, they logically distrust those systems and other service providers. In his examination of pathways to resilience among children who are system involved, Michael Ungar reports that "a negative placement experience in one system such as Child Welfare has been found to be directly related to a difficult placement history in another such as Mental Health" (2005a, 437).

Although some young people want to access the child welfare system, it is far more common to hear that they are actively trying to avoid being placed in that system. Some had already been in the child welfare system and "knew what [it] had to offer," "didn't have a good experience last time," and "didn't have any reason to think it would be a better experience this time" (J. Westmacott, personal communication, May 21, 2012). Among those with no prior child welfare involvement, the following sentiment is common: "He certainly did not want to have anything to do with [child welfare]. He didn't really have any [child welfare] experiences; he just wasn't open to it. I discussed the possibilities and what it would mean, and he just felt like there were too many possibilities to end up in a bad situation" (A. Kogel-Smucker, personal communication, May 22, 2012). Whether a young person has had prior experiences with child welfare or not, he or she largely does not think of it as a system that will change his or her experiences for the better.

Because youth want to remain outside the purview of child welfare, they often forsake the opportunity to receive other services. Some homeless youth prefer to stay on the streets or in less than ideal living situations with parents, guardians, and intimate partners than take the risk of entering a shelter and being brought to the attention of child welfare. Johanna Westmacott described the situation of one young cisgender woman: "She is a runaway from a group home right now, and she initially came here wanting to stay in our shelter. And the reason why she ultimately didn't . . . was because she wasn't 100 percent convinced that [child welfare] wouldn't find out that she was at the shelter, and that if there was any chance of that at all, she would figure something else out rather than go there" (personal communication, November 8, 2011). Food stamps are at the center of other examples of youth not receiving certain services out of fear of child welfare involvement. Although it is possible for youth to get their own food stamps, it requires them to prove that the person who is supposed to be providing for them is not. But proving that their guardian is not providing for them inevitably draws child welfare's attention to them. A young cisgender woman who just had a baby wanted to get her own food stamps. However, she opted not to pursue it because "it's a bigger priority to avoid [child welfare]," and she was certain that if she made a case to get her own food stamps, child welfare would question how she was able to take care of her baby and would ultimately take her child away from her (J. Melendez, personal communication, May 21, 2012).

PARENTS AND GUARDIANS

Because all of these young people are minors, case managers describe the ways in which interacting with clients' parents and guardians offers its own set of challenges. In some situations, these challenges mirror those seen in interactions between program staff and young people at the microsystem level. Like the young people described here, adult family members have had multiple experiences with service providers and are suspicious of their intent and ability to be of help (Davis 2003). When case managers make referrals that require a guardian to follow through, guardians sometimes fail to take the required next steps, so youth do not receive the services. Nicole Woodcox from STOP-IT in Chicago explained one such situation: "I've made referrals for various schools . . . because at one point in time [my client] said she wanted to get out of that school, and so [I] tried to get her involved with different schools. . . . [I] made the phone call; it was just left up to her and mom to finish it because I'm not her guardian. . . . I set that up for them and nothing happened" (personal communication, April 25, 2012). In other situations, guardians request certain services for their family, yet once a case manager makes the necessary arrangements, the guardian is no longer interested in the service.

Not unlike the competing priorities among young people, parents and guardians also have a great deal going on in their lives. For some adults, their own needs take precedent over their child's needs. Taking care of other children, dealing with their own mental health and substance use issues, and, for some, simply not being interested in helping their child and even wanting to sabotage their child are just some of the challenges that parents present to case managers when the case managers need the guardians' cooperation and involvement. Some parents are burned out and feel as if there is nothing they can do to help their child. Others are seemingly eager to hand over parental roles and responsibilities to the case manager. A case manager in Chicago recalled how a mother called her and communicated that her daughter had " 'been bad. She's been running away, and she asked me not to tell you because she wanted to get my trust again. But I'm telling you now because she's just, she's crossed the line. You need to do something with her.' And it was like, 'Why do you tell me now a month later that she actually hasn't been cooperating with you? And now you want me to fix it?' They're kind of looking at me as a disciplinarian" (N. Woodcox, personal communication, April 25, 2012).

The same problem in getting a child welfare worker to sign consent forms occurs with guardians. Statements such as "Her mom wouldn't sign the paperwork" and "Her mom would not cooperate, and so we couldn't get her connected with resources" illustrate this reality (E. Dalberg, personal communication, March 2, 2011). Guardians question certain services their child and case managers want and prevent their child from receiving those services.

Just as other service providers seemingly feel threatened by the case managers, so too do some guardians. This concern among guardians is often linked to their knowledge that case managers are mandated reporters and their fear that if they communicate with the case manager, that information will be used against them in a child welfare report (E. Dalberg, personal communication, March 2, 2011). In other situations, guardians view case managers as a direct threat to their expertise. One guardian "had experiences [working in] social services, and she saw us coming in as an insult to her and to her career and to her as a person because she thought that we were outsmarting her on her experience in social services" (A. Velasquez, personal communication, October 31, 2011).

These young people do not exist in isolation. For those who are still connected to their families, the challenge becomes how best to help the young person when their families also need support. Many case managers believe that unless they are able to effect some type of change within the family system, their clients' situation will not improve. As one case manager said, "I do take on the family role because I realize the client is not an island; I can't just help her and expect things to change for her if things don't change with the family" (N. Woodcox, personal communication, April 25, 2012).

JUVENILE JUSTICE SYSTEM

For programs that work closely with juvenile justice and law enforcement, especially in the form of mandated clients, the probation system offers unique collaborative challenges. Sporadic engagement with a program is very common among this group of young people. When clients who are involved in the juvenile justice system stop attending the mandated services, probation officers can be a point of contact for the case managers to assess the clients' situation. However, alerting a probation officer to the fact that clients have gone AWOL is "a very slippery slope because then if they're violating [the terms of their mandated services], and [the probation officer] is like, 'Oh, you don't know where they are?' then that might put them on the radar" (S. Larrea, personal communication, October 18, 2011). Therefore, case managers are reticent to contact probation officers out of concern that doing so might make matters worse for their clients.

Another point of tension between case managers and probation officers is how best to respond to young people's situations. When case managers are aware that their clients are going to be taken into custody, they can arrange for them to go into custody willingly and provide them with transportation. Sometimes, however, even though young people have agreed to such a scenario, probation officers disregard the agreement and do things on their own terms. In the case of a young cisgender woman in San Francisco, "The probation officer showed up at her house at 6:30 in the morning on a school day, asked the mom where my client was. [H]er mom said that she's in bed and asked if she should wake her up. [The probation officer] said, 'No, I want to wake her up from her bed,' and went into the house. . . . [M]y client's mother was very upset. . . . [M]y client was in her socks and wasn't even dressed, hadn't had breakfast, and the probation officer arrested her in front of another student and a former boyfriend of hers who was coming down to go to school and took her into custody" (P. Bagheri, personal communication, May 4, 2012). Such actions clearly make for strained relationships between probation officers and case managers. The case manager felt that this approach was "completely unnecessary. This client would have willingly gone into custody. She's a child; she hadn't had her breakfast; she should have been able to brush her teeth and go in with some dignity" (P. Bagheri, personal communication, May 4, 2012).

When juvenile justice officials question case managers' level of expertise, it can be difficult for the case managers to successfully advocate for their clients. Trying to collaborate with some attorneys evokes a hierarchy of perceived competence in which case managers are not considered strategic partners, and their input is not valued. In one such case, an attorney wanted to place a youth back in a home where she had been abused by her mother's boyfriend. Both the judge and attorney were confident that by issuing a restraining order against the boyfriend, the youth would be safe. Despite case managers' attempts to highlight the problems with this approach ("restraining orders don't mean much," and it was unlikely that the mother would abide by it because the man was the father of her two youngest children), the youth was placed back in the home. Very shortly after being back in the home, she ran away (P. Bagheri, personal communication, May 4, 2012). It is possible that if that attorney had listened to the case managers' input, this young cisgender woman would not have returned to the streets and to trading sex to survive.

In some instances, probation officers disagree with case managers about the types of services they feel will best serve their clients. This disagreement plays out when young people want to attend a specific school, and probation officers will not allow it because that specific school is not one typically used by the probation office. Young people who are trying to stop trading sex also sometimes request that they be allowed to attend residential programs outside of the county where they live. In the case of one such young cisgender woman, even though the residential director and her case manager supported this idea, "her probation officer opposed her going and said she wanted to take care of it 'in her own backyard'" (P. Bagheri, personal communication, May 4, 2012).

POLICE OFFICERS

Whether programs work closely with law enforcement officials or not, police officers pose unique challenges for programs who work with young people who trade sex. As explored in chapter 3, young people report routine physical and sexual abuse by police officers. It is therefore not surprising that they do not "consider the police to be a safety option or something that would increase [their] safety" (J. Westmacott, personal communication, May 22, 2012). Speaking about her interactions with police officers, Leah Albright-Byrd, a survivor of sex trafficking and executive director of Bridget's Dream, reflected, "I was exploited from 14 to 18 and in 4 years I did not have one encounter with law enforcement that could have led to my escape from my exploiter. I didn't have any encounters with law enforcement that invoked that sense of safety and empathy and warmth" (in Bullard and Wygal 2014). In addition to police officers' misconduct, the recognition that in most states these young people are engaged in criminalized behaviors reinforces their belief that the police cannot be utilized in times of need (Phillips et al. 2014). In their report about seeking legal remedies for criminalized trafficking victims, Suzannah Phillips and her colleagues address the collateral consequences of criminalization: "For individuals who have been trafficked into the sex trade, the threat of arrest and incarceration that permeates these proceedings can reinforce a fear of law enforcement and a belief that they cannot turn to law enforcement for help, because they are engaged in a criminalized sector" (2014, 19).

In the few cases where young people go to the police for help when they are victims of crimes, the police do not believe them and refuse to help them (P. Bagheri, personal communication, October 19, 2011; Iman et al. 2009; Williams 2010). A community-based participatory research project conducted by the Young Women's Empowerment Project in Chicago found that "police often accuse girls in the sex trade of lying or don't believe them when they turn to the police for help" (Iman et al. 2009, 30). The same is true when guardians try to file reports with the police. In one case, some cisgender men who were pimps came to a mother's house and got her daughter to leave with them. Even though the mother called the police and provided them with a description of the men and their license plate number, the police responded that her daughter probably just ran away from home and that they couldn't help her (P. Bagheri, personal communication, October 19, 2011).

An additional challenge in working with police is their seeming disregard for young people's specific safety needs. Police conduct interviews with youth at school even though a strong culture exists about not "snitching." A case manager in San Francisco explained how "when my client saw police coming into the school, she refused to talk to them because it doesn't really reflect well for kids to be talking to police at school" (P. Bagheri, personal communication, May 3, 2012). In the rare cases when a young person agreed to testify against a perpetrator, case managers expressed that they did not feel as if the police offered adequate protection for the youth. "You know, she was actually testifying against a serial rapist that was going around . . . and raping girls, and they caught him. . . . But the thing about it is they wanted her confession, but they didn't want to protect her in any type of way" (C. Roberts, personal communication, March 9, 2011).

When police officers operate in this manner, when they do not take young people's stories seriously, when they disregard parents' requests for help, and when they do not provide adequate protection for youth who are willing to assist in criminal cases, encouraging clients to work with law enforcement is a challenge for case managers. Because of police officers' illegal and unethical behavior with young people who trade sex, youth will be less likely to engage the services of and open up to case managers in a particular program if they know that a program works with law enforcement (Iman et al. 2009). Emi Koyama, activist and writer, explained at the 2014 Freedom Network Conference how some young people will not access services provided by a program that works closely with the police: "When they do these nationwide sweeps, they have a social worker riding along in their police cars so that they can offer services and resources. Now when a street youth sees that[,] they will think that, you know, well this social service organization is friends with cops, that means I am not going to feel safe there."

GUARDING TURF

Case managers are also prevented from assisting their clients when other social service providers view them as competitors who are infringing on their turf (Illback and Neil 1995; Johnson et al. 2003). When other providers feel that the case managers and their agencies are infringing on their turf, they will refuse to refer clients to them or will penalize clients who choose to access additional services elsewhere. In one case, a young cisgender woman was receiving services at two community-based organizations. One of the organizations called the other "and was kind of implying that we were keeping her away from them" (J. Melendez, personal communication, May 21, 2012). Over time this young person decided that she did want to access services at the first organization, but someone in this organization, feeling slighted by her initial disinterest in their services, "implied that she had her chance, and she chose [a different program]" (J. Westmacott, personal communication, May 21, 2012). Whereas prior to this exchange the young cisgender woman had been prioritized for housing with the first organization, she was told later that she would have to get on the wait list. In their interviews with stakeholders from state departments and private social service agencies, Lawrence Johnson and his colleagues also encountered the ways in which turf issues negatively affect clients. They describe how although competition among agencies can harm the agencies as well as the larger service delivery system, "[u]ltimately, the only losers are the clients served by the systems" (2003, 196).

ABSENCE OF SERVICES

Service providers who work with young people who trade sex agree that "too few services are available to meet current needs" (Institute of Medicine and the National Research Council 2013, 260). In general, urban areas do have social services available for young people who currently trade or formerly traded sex.[2] The services may not be specific to that population and may instead focus on points of overlap with other groups of young people, such as runaways and the homeless, LGBTQ, and youth who have been sexually abused, but the services nevertheless exist. Some providers argue that not all services are best equipped to provide specialized care for young people who trade sex (Institute of Medicine and the National Research Council 2013) and that specialized programs and services are needed (Finklea, Fernandes-Alcantara, and Siskin 2011; Reid 2010).

It is largely preferable to link young people to services in their geographic area. Even within urban areas where services are available, the geographic clustering of services within the city can prevent case managers from successfully linking a client to a requested service (Institute of Medicine and the National Research Council 2013). A young transgender woman in Chicago wanted to be connected with other transgender youth. Her case manager shared that even though "there are a couple really great organizations in Chicago, they're all in the Northside . . . [and the client] wasn't able to get to the Northside where the other great organizations are" (E. Knowles Wirsing, personal communication, March 2, 2011).

In less resource-rich locations, such as suburban and rural areas, the lack of services and the lack of appropriate services are major gaps that limit case managers' ability to be effective in their work with their clients (Koepplin and Pierce 2009; Pierce 2012). One young cisgender woman traveled approximately ninety minutes by bus to access counseling from a program because "she felt there were no appropriate services in the mental health realm" where she lived (S. Larrea, personal communication, March 8, 2011). Over time, the pressure of making this long commute became too much for her, especially because she was trying to maintain her other responsibilities of being a mother and attending school, so she stopped accessing mental health services entirely (P. Bagheri, personal communication, October 18, 2011). Because this young woman lived outside of the county where she accessed mental health services, it is possible that the case managers were not aware of resources in her home county. In areas where services are seemingly lacking, reaching out to providers of services for individuals involved in domestic violence and sexual assault situations may be a sustainable solution because most counties have these types of services, and "those types of organizations will be funded, forever" (Walker 2013b).

Even if services are available and accessible, they are not always the best fit for this group of young people who trade sex. In some instances, the young person in question differs significantly from a program's typical clients. In response to one young cisgender woman's request for tutoring in math, her case manager connected her with a tutoring program, but it didn't work out. "I don't know if it was the most appropriate program for her. . . . I was speaking to their director and people who work there, and I think that the young people they work with tend to come from a more privileged background and not the same culture as her in a lot of different ways, and they didn't seem really open to working with her" (J. Westmacott, personal communication, March 23, 2011). For those providers who have had limited to no exposure to young people who trade sex but are willing to work with them, case managers explain how they have "well-meaning and well-intentioned efforts" yet are not equipped to work with this population (P. Bagheri, personal communication, May 3, 2012).

COMPETING PRIORITIES

A key challenge when case managers attempt to work with other providers and systems is the various groups' differing philosophical values that influence their organizational agendas and hoped-for outcomes (Glisson and James 1992; Hodges, Nesman, and Hernandez 1999; Illback and Neill 1995; Kagan 1993; Meyers 1993; Ungar 2005b). Systems are "often as concerned with meeting their mandates uncritically as they are addressing the needs of children in ways meaningful to them [the children]" (Ungar 2005b, 450). As mentioned earlier, law enforcement wants to see these young people participate in trials and be witnesses. Case managers want their clients to be safe and are concerned about the ways in which their cooperation with law enforcement jeopardizes their safety. Judge Fernando Comacho of Queens County, New York, speaks to this tension: "[T]he advocates want the kids to be safe, they want them to get out of the life, but they don't want them to cooperate with law enforcement against the pimps because they fear for the kids' safety and rightly so. On the law enforcement side, on the D.A. side, on the police side, they want these kids to cooperate and be witnesses. They may not be as concerned about their safety as the advocates are. So there's always been that inherent conflict" (in Schweig 2012).

Structuring social services for or providing them to young people in hopes that they will become better witnesses in legal cases "creates this different philosophical attitude about how the services should be delivered" (Koyama 2014). In such cases, youth are provided with services not because they simply deserve them but because providers hope to get something out of them. Speaking at the Conference to End Child Sex Trafficking in 2013, Maureen French, victim–witness coordinator for the U.S. Attorney's Office, confirmed this prioritization of making someone a good witness: "Once cases are on board, without the victims testifying you are not going to have much of a case. So you really need those victims to be there. So the services we provide are really to make sure that the victim is in good mental health condition, they have a home to go to, and things like that. . . . We take the victim where they're at, and then we connect them up with community resources so they are able to be empowered and have the ability to come and provide testimony." With this commitment to prosecution, however, the measured outcomes are no longer to achieve the young person's stability and to meet his or her self-identified needs.

For interagency coordination of services to occur, intraorganizational functioning is imperative. Studies about the intraorganizational climate of social service agencies have found that many agencies are characterized by poor worker attitudes, time pressures, resource limitations, high rates of employee turnover, low job satisfaction, and role disagreement (Glisson and Durick 1988; Illback and Neill 1995; Lipsky 1980; Smith and Donovan 2003; Soloman 1986; Ungar 2005b). These conditions within the organizational culture inhibit individuals' ability to adhere to best-practice ideals (Lipsky 1980). When individual agencies and systems are "turbulent, poorly led and resourced" (Horwath and Morrison 2007, 60), it is not surprising that interagency collaboration is difficult.

To best meet the needs of young people who trade sex, greater coordination of services is needed. Young people who trade sex present with a complex array of service needs, including very basic needs such as food, clothing, and transportation as well as needs for mental, physical, and sexual health services. Because many of these young people cross multiple service sectors, including child welfare and juvenile justice, coordination of care is often disjointed and fragmented. Some agencies are reluctant (or even unwilling) to share information, which leads to service delays and potentially a duplication of services. In addition, because many of these young people want to avoid the child welfare system, they are adamant about not accessing certain services such as education, housing, and food stamps for fear of being reported. Perceived competition strains collaborations and limits case managers' ability to meet their clients' needs. Parents feel threatened by case managers and stall efforts to connect their children with requested services. Child welfare workers reprimand case managers for being too involved in their clients' lives. Probation officers and attorneys question case managers' expertise to the detriment of youth.

Across systems, providers are in agreement that youth who trade sex need services. Despite this common understanding, each system has its own unique philosophical orientation to this social issue, resulting in clashes between the various systems (Illback and Neill 1995). Likewise, interagency collaboration is clouded by tensions associated with turf issues, which must be addressed for any collaboration to be successful (Hodges, Nesman, and Hernandez 1999; Johnson et al. 2003). In their examination of interorganizational service coordination, Charles Glisson and Anthony Hemmelgarn found that successful collaboration requires "caseworkers to be responsive to unexpected problems and individualized needs, tenacious in navigating the complex bureaucratic maze of state and federal regulations, and able to form personal relationships that win the trust and confidence of a variety of children and families" (1988, 404). For interagency collaboration to be effective, equal commitment among partners, specification of shared goals, the development of trust, recognition of strengths and limitations, and ongoing, consistent communication are needed (Hodges, Nesman, and Hernandez 1999; Huxham and Vaugen 2000; Whetton 1981).

Several ways exist to resolve some of the mesolevel challenges that prevent youth's needs from being met. Eve Birge, the liaison on domestic human trafficking for the U.S. Department of Education, suggests that "solutions are far from easy and require that many systems change and they really do require some collaboration and very new ways of working together with regard to these systems" (in Birge et al. 2013). Youth should not be prevented from accessing services because their guardians are not capable of signing consent forms. Situations where young people want to get their own food stamps but do not pursue the process because they want to avoid child welfare may also be preventable. All of the potential solutions to these types of challenges require policy changes and therefore are explored in chapter 7 in connection with macrosystem challenges.

6

FROM CRIMINALIZATION TO DECRIMINALIZATION

LOCAL RESPONSES TO DOMESTIC MINOR SEX TRAFFICKING

Although the TVPA classifies youth who trade sex as sex trafficking victims, the act is limited in its applicability because prostitution-related offenses are regulated by the individual states and not by the federal government. It is rare that local prostitution cases fall under federal jurisdiction; therefore, the TVPA is read as largely inapplicable for young people detained for prostitution offenses (Lynch and Widner 2008). Therefore, in the majority of states young people involved in sex trades are still being arrested and charged.

This chapter first examines prostitution arrest trends since the passage of the TVPA. In reviewing these data, it shows that the victim approach set forth by the TVPA has not trickled down to the state level. These data also indicate the ways in which notions of victims are produced. After a discussion of the politics of victimhood, the chapter turns its attention to the ways in which California, Illinois, and New York specifically are responding to young people who trade sex.

ARREST RATES

Arrest rates since the TVPA's enactment in 2000 reveal the discrepancy between federal and local approaches. Despite the federal classification of young people involved in sex trades as domestic minor victims of human trafficking, prostitution-related arrests increased the first ten years after the TVPA was enacted (see table 6.1).[1] Although the overall number of arrests of young people decreased by 20 percent during this period, the number of

TABLE 6.1 TEN-YEAR PROSTITUTION ARREST TRENDS FOR MINORS, 2000-2009

OFFENSES CHARGED	2000	2009	% CHANGE
Total arrests	1,455,216	1,161,830	−20.20
Prostitution and commercialized vice	729	791	8.50

SOURCE: DATA COMPILED BY THE AUTHOR FROM U.S. FBI 2010B, TABLE 33.

arrests for prostitution and commercialized vice increased 8.5 percent (U.S. FBI 2010a).

When data for 2009 through 2013 are included (table 6.2), we find that for the first fourteen years of the TVPA, arrests of young people for prostitution-related offenses decreased nearly 25 percent (U.S. FBI 2014a). Later in this chapter I consider how this transition from an increase to a decrease in arrests may reflect the emerging trend of charging young people with offenses other than prostitution-related ones.

An examination of arrest rates by biological sex helps us better understand what is happening with prostitution-related arrests (table 6.3). In the ten-year period after the TVPA was enacted, arrest rates for prostitution decreased nearly 50 percent for boys even though arrest rates for all offenses decreased by only 30 percent. Although overall arrest rates for young women decreased by 13 percent during this period, prostitution arrests of young women increased by 57 percent (U.S. FBI 2010a).

If we include data provided for the years 2010 through 2013, we still see the sexual double standard of prostitution-related arrests of young people. Figure 6.1 shows the yearly prostitution-related arrests by biological sex since the passage of the TVPA in 2000. Through 2013, the number of young men arrested for prostitution-related offenses has continued to decrease at a rate higher than their arrests for all offenses (69 percent versus 55 percent). From

TABLE 6.2 FOURTEEN-YEAR PROSTITUTION ARREST TRENDS FOR MINORS, 2000-2013

OFFENSES CHARGED	2000	2013	% CHANGE
Total arrests	1,455,216	666,263	−54.22
Prostitution and commercialized vice	729	550	−24.55

SOURCE: DATA COMPILED BY THE AUTHOR FROM U.S. FBI 2010B, TABLE 33.

TABLE 6.3 TEN-YEAR PROSTITUTION ARREST TRENDS FOR MINORS BY SEX, 2000-2009

OFFENSES CHARGED	MALE			FEMALE		
	2000	2009	% CHANGE	2000	2009	% CHANGE
Total arrests	1,047,690	807,818	−22.9	407,526	354,012	−13.1
Prostitution and commercialized vice	729	550	−24.55	397	624	57.2

SOURCE: DATA COMPILED BY THE AUTHOR FROM U.S. FBI 2010B, TABLE 33.

2009 through 2012, the number of young women arrested for prostitution-related offenses decreased. In 2013, however, a 5 percent increase in prostitution-related arrests for young women occurred. Based on 2013 data, the arrest rates for young women are 12 percent higher than they were when the TVPA was first enacted in 2000. This is true even though the overall arrest rates for young women decreased by 53 percent during this time period.

The arrest rates indicate how the victim approach established in the TVPA has been slow to permeate state-level responses. This finding is also demon-

FIGURE 6.1 YEARLY U.S. PROSTITUTION ARREST TRENDS FOR MINORS BY BIOLOGICAL SEX.

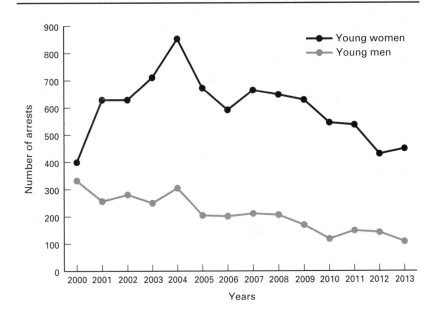

strated by the work of Operation Cross Country, the cross-country sweeps conducted by the Innocence Lost National Initiative. The FBI (2014c) reports that since their inception the cross-country sweeps have rescued 3,400 children from the sex industry. But the arrest data from 2003–2012 (figure 6.1) show that 8,177 young people were arrested nationwide for prostitution-related charges. The number will clearly be much higher once data from 2013 and 2014 are released. Similarly, a stark difference exists between arrest data and human trafficking offense data collected by the FBI's UCR program.[2] In 2013, 550 young people were arrested for prostitution-related charges, but none were listed as victims of human trafficking involving commercial sex acts (U.S. FBI 2015). This large discrepancy begs the question of why even though some of these young people are considered victims, at the local level between 58 and 100 percent more of them are being arrested and treated like criminals. The response to my query about the FBI's UCR data provides some insight. Whoever responds to inquiries sent to the email address provided on the FBI UCR guidance form for monthly returns of human trafficking offenses known to law enforcement wrote the following: "A minor can be a prostitute and not a victim of HT [human trafficking]. Therefore the number of juvenile prostitutes will not match the number of HT [commercial sex acts] incidents" (personal communication, February 3, 2015).[3] Stephen G. Fischer Jr., chief of Multimedia Productions for the FBI Criminal Justice Information Services Divisions, clarified that "a juvenile could be [a] prostitute in situations where the john [client], or even the pimp, did not recklessly disregard the age of the prostitute and there is no force, fraud, or coercion involved. Essentially, the prostitute is an older juvenile who looks like an adult, has identification as an adult, and/or is in a location that is for adults only" (personal communication, February 27, 2015). This response reflects the differential state categorization of young people involved in trading sex as delinquents or victims. It also reflects subjective ideas about who is truly a victim (Annitto 2011).[4]

"IDEAL VICTIMS"

Research that focuses broadly on youth interactions with police officers has found that younger youth are responded to more leniently than are their old-

er counterparts (McEachern and Bauzer 1967; Morash 1984) and that the decision to arrest a young person is greatly influenced by the youth's demeanor
(Black 1980; Lundman 1996a, 1996b) and prior criminal record (Gottfredson
and Gottfredson 1988). Police responses to younger youth reflect the belief
"that young children are less mature and therefore are less culpable for their
actions" (Halter 2010, 153) and that victims are passive, vulnerable individuals (Quinney 1972; Von Hentig 1948).

The findings from recent work in the United States that examined factors associated with law enforcement officials viewing young people who
trade sex as victims reflect those of the larger literature.[5] Three studies that
reviewed juvenile prostitution case files found that those youth whose involvement in trading sex come to the attention of the police through a report
rather than from police action and those who have a third-party exploiter
are more likely to be considered victims (Halter 2010; Mitchell, Finkelhor,
and Wolak 2010; Wells, Mitchell, and Ji 2012). In her review of case files from
six police agencies in major U.S. cities, Stephanie Halter explains that "the
fact that the police almost always consider reported youth as victims suggests that the police accept the innocent victim status denoted by the report-
er seeking police aid . . . [and that] 'complicit' youth are more challenging
for the police" (2010, 157). Other factors associated with being viewed as a
victim include being female, having a history of running away from home,
being younger than sixteen, and appearing frightened (Mitchell, Finkelhor,
and Wolak 2010). Furthermore, those who cooperate with law enforcement
or who do not have a prior arrest record are also more likely to be considered
victims (Halter 2010). Young people who either do not have or do not provide police with a third party to blame or who in other ways seem complicit
in their involvement trading sex are more likely to be considered culpable
and thus to be arrested.

Because juvenile justice case files do not indicate whether a young person
identifies as transgender, we cannot be sure to what extent law enforcement
views young transgender individuals as victims. However, with the findings
from studies that 90 to 100 percent of all transgender young people in their
samples have histories of arrest (Curtis et al. 2008; Garofalo et al. 2006) and
that young transgender women are frequently arrested for prostitution-related offenses even when they are not working (Curtis et al. 2008), there is con-
siderable support for the idea that they would not be viewed as victims. In

the eyes of the law, it appears that only young cisgender women involved in sex trades are considered victims. This gendered approach to victimhood is reminiscent of the stereotypical images of "helpless young women and girls, forced into prostitution" (Chang and Kim 2007, 343) that arose with the historical concept of white slavery given in the Mann Act. It may also reflect the juvenile justice system's response to girls' sexual activity.

To understand the current legal responses to young people involved in sex trades, it is first important to examine the juvenile justice system's underlying philosophical goals. The first juvenile justice court was founded in Cook County, Illinois, in 1899. The court justices felt that youth were not criminals. They instead viewed society as the criminal because it allowed the social conditions to exist in which these young people found themselves in trouble with the law (Schwartz 2009). The earliest form of the juvenile justice system was guided by two philosophies. It was interventionist in that it sought to create programs that would rescue young people from crime and truancy. At the same time, it was also diversionary and wanted to prevent young people from entering the criminal courts. In the late nineteenth and early twentieth centuries, however, it was young women who were most often charged with immorality or incorrigibility. Guiding these charges was the belief that if girls were not incarcerated for this type of behavior, they would continue their promiscuity to the detriment of their morality (Schwartz 2009).

This tension around sex remains and is still found in the response to youth, in particular young cisgender women, involved in sex trades. Law enforcement officials currently claim that it is for a young woman's own good that they are arresting her—that if they did not arrest her, they would not be able to link her to services she desperately needs or to build a criminal case against third parties (Ball 2005; Halter 2010; Mitchell, Finkelhor, and Wolak 2010). Chief Deputy District Attorney Teresa Lowry of the Juvenile Division in the Clark County District Attorney's Office, Las Vegas, Nevada, explained this approach: "Our concern is, are [juvenile offenders] a danger to themselves or a danger to the community? . . . [T]hey're clearly a danger to themselves. Physical assaults, beatings, sexual abuse, venereal diseases, pregnancy, psychological damage—the risks are tremendous. . . . [Detention protects the girls and] allows the cops to come talk to them so we can pursue prosecution of the adult offender" (qtd. in Ball 2005). This gendered notion of victimhood relies on the conception of female weakness and brings with it judgments about female sexuality and sexual agency.[6] Thus, the contemporary juvenile justice system shares with its historical predecessor the desire to save girls. This goal pervades the consciousness not just of juvenile judges, prosecutors, and advocates but also of the larger community (Schwartz 2009).

Social control agents—the police, social service providers, health professionals—are the ones most frequently involved in defining who is worthy of victim status (Aradau 2004; Holstein and Miller 1990). Once ascribed, victim status is indicative of the belief that individuals are not responsible for their fates, are incapable of taking care of themselves, and require the intervention of social control agents (Loseke and Cahill 1984). An "ideal victim" is "a person or category of individuals who—when hit by a crime—most readily are given the complete and legitimate status of being a victim" (Christie 1986, 18). It comes as no surprise, then, that among young people who trade sex, those who fit stereotypical notions of childhood, such as helplessness, innocence, and dependence, have an increased likelihood of being considered victims. Author and activist Tara Burns details what she has learned are the rules for being a good victim: "Apparently there are rules for being a good victim: 1) Victims should cry. 2) They should talk about horrible things done to them by criminals, but not by the police. 3) They should not have opinions, and 4) [i]f they do have opinions, they should present themselves as traumatized enough so that those opinions are easily discountable. If victims don't behave this way, their status as victims can be called into question" (2014).

Victim status is discretionary and reflects whose suffering and what suffering are deemed worthy of attention. The "hierarchy of victimization" is reinforced by mainstream media representations of very young cisgender girls forced into trading sex (Greer 2007). These representations of "ideal victims" (Christie 1986) leave middle-class notions of respectability, gender, and innocence unexamined. They reflect the gendered stereotype of "girls as soft, passive, fragile, and in need of intervention and support, but boys as hard and tough, able to take care of themselves" (Dennis 2008, 21). Ultimately, "we have what is considered a legitimate victim and an illegitimate victim. That's a problem" (Dang 2014). When young people seem complicit in their involvement, and when they do not cooperate with law enforcement, they assume an argentic position that runs counter to ideas about the relative powerlessness of children, making it difficult for them to be viewed as victims.

This "politics of pity" (Aradau 2004, 254) fosters an environment where "some suffering is recognized and some goes unnoticed" and where "those who are recognized as suffering must also be deemed deserving" (Walklate 2012, 179). It is therefore not surprising that cisgender boys, transgender youth, and young people who are not forced by a third party to trade sex remain outside the purview of victim status. They are not seen to be innocent and thus are not deserving of pity. To include them would require an alternative theory of reality where both "those who threaten [social] order and those who suffer because of that order" are included in the social construction of victims (Quinney 1972, 321). Such a shift, Richard Quinney explains, would allow the "rhetoric of victimization" (1972, 315) to conceive of victims more broadly; it would no longer be limited to individual-level violence and specific to people who are deemed worthy of protecting. Such a "radical victimology makes visible the power relations that underpin who is seen and responded to as a victim and who is not, and thus affords a much wider and far-reaching conceptualization of what counts as crime" (Walklate 2012, 175).

INDIVIDUAL STATE RESPONSES

In attempts to align state-level responses to young people's involvement in sex trades more closely with the federal definition of sex trafficking of domestic minors in the TVPA, states have developed their own local approaches. Three states—California, Illinois, and New York—represent the range of local responses that currently exist in the United States.

CALIFORNIA: CRIMINALIZATION

Starting at the age of eighteen, a person can legally consent to sex in California. However, any person regardless of age can be charged for violating section 647(b) of the California Penal Code,[7] which classifies prostitution as disorderly conduct and specifies that anyone who agrees to engage in or engages in any act of prostitution is guilty of disorderly conduct, a misdemeanor. Section 647(b) clearly cannot be reconciled with the statutory rape law that defines the age of consent.

Although involvement in sex trades is thus a criminal offense for youth, California has passed a significant amount of legislation focused on domestic minor sex trafficking. In 2005, Assembly Bill 22 established human trafficking as a felony crime, and in cases where minors are involved the penalty is four, six, or eight years in state prison.[8] This bill also permits victims to bring civil action against their traffickers, and it established an interagency statewide task force.

The majority of subsequent California legislation continues to target third parties and clients, with proceeds earmarked for service provision. In 2009, Assembly Bill 17 was enacted; it classifies as criminal profiteering any cases involving the trafficking of minors for prostitution or fraudulently inducing a minor into prostitution.[9] Additional fines for the procurement of a child younger than sixteen can be up to $20,000. Any proceeds made from forfeiting property and fines are to be deposited into the Victim–Witness Assistance Fund. The money from the fund is allocated for counseling programs that serve sexually abused or exploited youth. Bill 17 requires that 50 percent of the funds be given to community-based organizations that work with minor victims of trafficking.

Two bills enacted at the beginning of 2012 are also illustrative of legislation that targets third parties and clients. Assembly Bill 12, the Abolition of Child Commerce, Exploitation, and Sexual Slavery Act, allows courts to impose an additional fine on individuals convicted of soliciting or acquiring the sexual services of a person younger than eighteen.[10] The fine can be up to $25,000 and is earmarked to fund programs and services for commercially sexually exploited minors. Assembly Bill 90 adds to the definition of criminal profiteering activity set forth in the California Control of Profits of Organized Crime Act the offense of inducing a minor to engage in commercial sex by use of force, coercion, threat, fear, or injury to the minor or to another person.[11] Any proceeds from the property forfeited in these cases are deposited in the Victim–Witness Assistance Fund.

In the November 2012 election, California residents overwhelmingly voted in favor of Proposition 35, the Californians Against Sexual Exploitation (CASE) Act.[12] The CASE Act increases the penalties associated with child sex trafficking set forth by Assembly Bill 22 from four to eight years in state prison to five to twelve years. Monetary fines associated with the crime of child sex trafficking can be up to $500,000 with an optional additional penalty of up to $1 million. These fines are placed in the Victim–Witness Assistance Fund. Anyone convicted of being a sex trafficker is mandated to register as a sex offender for the rest of their lives. The provision that convicted traffickers have to inform law enforcement anytime they register with an Internet service provider or change an Internet identifier even if their crime did not involve the Internet was successfully challenged by the American Civil Liberties Union and the Electronic Freedom Foundation for being overly broad and violating citizens' rights. California attorney general Kamala Harris indicated that her office intends to rewrite the Internet-disclosure requirement to meet the court's objections (Egelko 2015). Last, police officers assigned to field or investigative duties are required to receive a two-hour training about human trafficking.

ILLINOIS: DECRIMINALIZATION

The Illinois Safe Children Act, signed into law in 2010, is the first enacted state legislation that is in compliance with the TVPA and provides new protections to young people involved in trading sex.[13] It decriminalized minors' involvement in sex trades by transferring their jurisdiction from the criminal justice system to the child protection system. Because children cannot consent to commercial sex, references to "juvenile prostitutes" have been removed from the criminal code. These young people are to be viewed as victims of human trafficking, not as juvenile offenders. The act also limits traffickers' and clients' defense that they thought the individual was eighteen to those instances where the defendants had no reasonable opportunity to see the young person (Cook County State's Attorney's Office 2010). Furthermore, it created new categories in the definition of the term *abused child* in the Abused and Neglected Child Reporting Act and in the definition of the term *abused minor* in the Juvenile Court Act. These redefinitions overcome the exclusion of cases that involve other third-party perpetrators or youth acting on their own accord in most child protection laws directed at child maltreatment (i.e., child abuse or child neglect) perpetrated by a parent, caretaker, or guardian. Finally, the act charges the Illinois Department of Children and Family Services (DCFS) with the responsibility of identifying and serving young people who trade sex (Walts et al. 2011).

The child welfare system has been suggested as the public agency best equipped to respond to young people who trade sex (Brittle 2008) because it is already mandated to work with vulnerable and marginalized children (Goldman et al. 2003). The overrepresentation of minors in the child welfare system who are at high risk for trading sex (Kotrla 2010) also suggests opportunities for identifying those previously unreported as involved in sex trades. However, the child welfare system requires substantial support to meet this challenge, including training, development of screening protocols, and resources for response.

Illinois DCFS has engaged in extensive capacity building in response to its mandate within the act. To meet the needs of young people referred by law enforcement and current wards of the agency who are at high risk of involvement in trading sex, it has promised that all staff will have the necessary tools to understand, identify, and respond to young people involved in sex trades. These protocols are described in the report *Building a Child Welfare Response to Child Trafficking* (known as *The Blueprint*), developed by DCFS and the International Organization for Adolescents (Walts et al. 2011) .

The Blueprint is both a training manual and a set of practice resources for child welfare workers who are either responding to referrals for those young people who are suspected of being involved in sex trades or conducting reviews for youth in DCFS custody. It delineates the DCFS approach to integrating these young people into its agency mandate. It also recognizes the importance of systematic screening and assessment in the success of identification of this population. Included in *The Blueprint* are screening and assessment tools, including indicator checklists, guidance for how to interview young people, and rapid and comprehensive screening forms. *The Blueprint* also delineates best practices for case management of young people involved in sex trades. As of 2014, no validity checks have been performed on *The Blueprint*.

NEW YORK: THE PARTIAL DECRIMINALIZATION MODEL

The New York Safe Harbour for Exploited Children Act (SHA) allows young people arrested for prostitution to defer criminal prosecution by petitioning for consideration as a person in need of supervision (PINS) (Meisner 2009;

Schwartz 2009).[14] This proactive attempt in New York to protect rather than to prosecute young people involved in sex trades was passed in 2008 and enacted in April 2010. A PINS classification provides an opportunity for child welfare services to achieve jurisdiction over the young person and to mandate that person to services that, it is hoped, will facilitate his or her transition away from sex trades.

The SHA amends the New York Social Services Law to enhance the role of child protection services in providing support and services to these youth. Every local social services district is mandated to address this population's child welfare needs, and if funds are available, all districts are to make sure that preventative services such as safe housing and community-based programs are available. To ensure law enforcement participation, the local commissioner of each district provides training to help law enforcement officials identify these young people and help connect them with services. In addition, the Office of Children and Family Services must contract with a nonprofit organization that has experience working with youth involved in sex trades to operate at least one safe house in the state. The staff of the safe house must receive training about how to best work with these young people and must directly or indirectly provide the continuum of services that this population needs (Meisner 2009). The idea is that a system that allows these youth to have access to emergency housing, medical care, and therapeutic and educational services will better facilitate their transitions back into the community.

At first glance, the SHA reflects the TVPA's definition that all young people involved in sex trades are victims of a severe form of human trafficking. Upon closer examination, we see that the SHA does not decriminalize prostitution for all young people.

As a result of the SHA, prostitution is decriminalized for some young people. An examination of the PINS provisions reveals which youth are still subject to criminal prosecution. The first group of young people not covered by the PINS comprises those who are sixteen or seventeen years old. In its original form, the SHA limited PINS eligibility to youth younger than sixteen. In 2014, the New York State Legislature amended the criminal procedure law to allow those who are sixteen and seventeen to be eligible to receive the range of services for sexually exploited youth available under the SHA. But this amendment still allows these young people to be arrested for prostitution-related offenses, "processed through the criminal justice system, and treated

as criminals" (Phillips et al. 2014, 12). Also excluded from a PINS classification are young people who have previously committed prostitution. Youth
previously classified as a PINS as well as those who express unwillingness
to cooperate with the mandated specialized services for sexually exploited
youth are also excluded from a PINS classification. Finally, if a young person
orders a PINS petition and then does not comply with the conditions im-
posed, the court may reestablish the delinquency procedures.

In 2010, New York became the first state to enact a vacatur remedy. This
remedy allows the erasure of prostitution-related offenses from the records of
victims of human trafficking, including young people who trade sex. Vacating convictions is an important step in allowing young people to clear certain
criminal convictions they received while they were technically crime victims.
Since 2010, a total of 369 convictions have been vacated for thirty-eight people
(minors and adults) (Mogulesco 2014). The American Bar Association passed
a resolution supporting the vacating of convictions and recommends that
such vacatur remedies should be made available nationwide (Baskin 2014b).

CRITICAL ANALYSIS OF STATE RESPONSE

Despite the TVPA's classification of all domestic youth who trade sex as victims of sex trafficking, in New York and California young people are still being arrested for prostitution-related offenses. UCR data for 2013 reveals that
205 prostitution arrests of minors occurred in California, and 22 in New
York (U.S. FBI 2014b). In the case of Illinois, where juvenile prostitution has
been decriminalized, young people, surprisingly, are still being arrested. In
2013, UCR data shows that 8 prostitution of arrests of minors were reported
by Illinois (U.S. FBI 2014b). What is more common is for young people in
Illinois to be charged with other offenses instead. In some cases, police officers are initially charging them with prostitution-related offenses because
they are unaware of the change in the law. Even though young people can
still be arrested in California for prostitution-related offenses, in some
counties, such as San Francisco, the unofficial policy is not to charge them
with prostitution offenses. In one situation, a young cisgender woman was
arrested in California for prostitution and during the arrest lied and said
she was eighteen. Once it came to the authorities' attention that she was a

minor, she no longer faced a prostitution charge; rather, she was charged with lying to a police officer. Her case manager in San Francisco explained the situation: "The probation officer's response was that, 'Well, in our eyes she's not a victim; in our eyes she's a criminal because she lied to the police.' And that's her charge. The charge that stuck was lying to a police officer about her name, about her identity when she was rescued, which is how the pimps, you know, that's exactly what they're coached to do, it's exactly what she was told to do. . . . There she was held in custody for over two months, over two and a half months . . . supposedly for her own safety" (P. Bagheri, personal communication, May 4, 2012).

Similar to the gendered prostitution arrest rates for young people, this idea of holding young people, in particular young cisgender women, "for their own good" is another example of the gender bias inherent in the juvenile justice system (Sherman 2012) and the "detention-to-protection pipeline" (Musto 2013). Minh Dang highlights how framing "trafficking as a crime versus a human rights violation" makes it "a criminal justice response" wherein "people justify arresting people for the sake of services" (personal communication, January 16, 2014). Furthermore, with an emphasis on prosecution, people are "rarely seen as the holders of rights. They are instead seen as 'instruments' in investigations or prosecution" (Craggs and Martens 2010, 49). Detective John Sydow of the Sacramento County Sherriff's Office indicated that even when attempts are made to link people to appropriate services, for the criminal justice system the benefit of doing so is that a more stable victim "makes a better witness" (qtd. in Bullard and Wygal 2014). Criminalization unfortunately exacerbates rather than alleviates the problems these young people experience.

Neither the TVPA nor its subsequent reauthorizations in 2003, 2005, 2008, and 2013 nor the local responses address the root factors that contribute to young people either deciding that sex trades are their best option or finding themselves in a situation where they are forced or coerced to engage in these behaviors.[15] Indeed, the root causes of criminalized behaviors cannot easily be changed, especially by the government (J. Wilson 1975). California's approach in maintaining the criminalization of youth's involvement in trading sex, although increasing the penalties associated with solicitation offenses involving minors, is questionable. This rational approach to deviance—the idea that if we simply make the punishments severe enough, people will stop engaging in the prohibited behavior—has limited validity (Denzin 1990; Pfohl 1994; Tittle 1969). It has failed in the war on drugs, and it will also fail when applied to the issue of young people who trade sex. In his interpretive reading of rational choice theory, Norman Denzin explains, "For a rational choice to be made, an actor knows how an end affects other plans, knows the desirable and undesirable consequences of any given means, or set of ends, knows the different chains of means that are available at any given moment, and knows how these means affect other means and goals" (1990, 174). Such a rational actor does not exist and is based on the misguided assumption that everyone shares a similar rational calculus (Pfohl 1994). Speaking out against California Proposition 35 on a panel at Stanford University, John Vanek, a retired police lieutenant in San Jose, California, argued: "Californians against Slavery started with the assumption, the presumption, that raising sentencing would impact crime. That just doesn't work. Get on Google, do the research. Raising sentencing is not a crime prevention tactic. If it [is], we wouldn't have drug problems, would we? These are very, very complex issues" (2012).

Another limitation of increased penalties against third parties is that they may prevent young people from receiving restitution when they have been forced to trade sex. Looking to Proposition 35 in California, the increased criminal penalties of $500,000, with an optional additional fine of up to $1 million, do not go directly to the victim. Monies from criminal cases are instead placed in the Victim–Witness Assistance Fund, which is distributed to law enforcement agencies and anti-trafficking social service organizations. What this means is that if youth pursue a civil case, where any monetary fines go directly to them, it is unlikely that the defendants will have any remaining financial resources. The only way young people can then benefit from proceeds gathered in criminal cases is if they access services from agencies who are awarded this money.

Reminiscent of how the Mann Act resulted in women and girls being charged and convicted as co-conspirators, an increasing collateral consequence of a criminal justice response to young people who trade sex is that the young people who are purportedly victims of crimes are once again being charged as co-conspirators of their own trafficking (Dorsey 2013; Locke 2014; Mogulesco 2014; R. Richardson 2014) and are having to register as sex offenders (Mogulesco 2014). It is not surprising that an emphasis on prosecution rather than on prevention or protection results in an increase of problematic prosecutions. Robin Richardson, Equal Justice Fellow at the Urban Justice Center's Sex Workers Project, explained the incentives for prosecution during the annual Freedom Network Conference in 2014:

> Few incentives exist right now for prosecutors to not prosecute victims of human trafficking as co-conspirators. There are a couple of incentives to con-vict victims, or at least to charge them. One, you can hold that charge over a victim's head and say if you do not cooperate with me, I will convict you as a co-conspirator, which is actually pretty easy when you consider how broad the federal conspiracy law is. It's just one act in furtherance of a crime. The second reason why it might be advantageous for somebody to convict some-one is it does boost numbers. You can catch two instead of one trafficker, at least on the books. (2014)

In states such as California where a human-trafficking conviction results in lifetime registry as a sex offender, the collateral consequences of being charged as a co-conspirator are severe.

The United Nations expressed its concern about these collateral conse-quences for trafficking victims in its periodic review of the United States on this issue. The summary document from that review directs that "the State party should take all appropriate measures to prevent the criminalization of victims of sex trafficking, including child victims, insofar as they have been compelled to engage in unlawful activities" (U.S. Human Rights Network 2014, 7). When young people who trade sex, all of whom are considered vic-tims of sex trafficking by federal law, are convicted as traffickers, they not only "have the extra injury of being a co-conspirator with [their] trafficker [but also] have the extra stigma that will bar [them] from a lot of services for victims of trafficking even though [they] are victims" (R. Richardson 2014).

The issue of young people involved in sex trades will not be solved by ar-resting and prosecuting them. For some young people, court intervention can lead to positive changes; for others, it can exacerbate conditions such as poverty and trauma (Brown, Rodriguez, and Smith 2010). Nonetheless, arresting and prosecuting young people send the dual message that they are both victims and criminals. Because prostitution laws cannot be reconciled with statutory rape laws that define the age of consent, it is inappropriate to charge young people with prostitution-related offenses. Furthermore, the legislation that increases penalties for solicitation of minors does not grant youth social and economic power and does not acknowledge their needs and desires. Without this power, young people are still at risk for becoming involved in sex trades regardless of the increased penalties for third parties and clients. As Ambassador Luis CdeBaca in the U.S. Department of State Office to Monitor and Combat Trafficking in Persons stated, "You can't prosecute your way out of this problem. You can't even legislate your way out of this problem" (qtd. in Kovtun 2013).

The negative effects of criminalizing young people's involvement in trading sex are far worse than any positive gains it may create. The legal approach used in California and New York are forms of secondary victimization. In both locations, the very system that is supposed to protect these young people is victimizing them by arresting them. No work to date has shown that arresting people "for their own good" is helpful the majority of the time (Brown, Rodriguez, and Smith 2010) or that pressing charges against a young person facilitates his or her cooperation in building cases against third parties. Criminalization results in discriminatory enforcement patterns, as witnessed by the disproportionate number of girls arrested for prostitution-related offenses as compared to the number of boys arrested. It also encourages social control agents to abuse their power (Pfohl 1994). Some police physically and sexually abuse young people involved in sex trades.

Although trainings created specifically for law enforcement are needed, training programs are only as good as their content. The training video that was created as a result of California Proposition 35 (Bullard and Wygall 2014) makes it clear that the more complicated nature of this issue remains unexamined. The video training does not address the ways in which some police officers abuse their power and further exploit young people. The training focuses exclusively on young cisgender women who have a third party forcing them to trade sex. No guidance is offered on how to work with LGBTQ young people, young cisgender men, or young people who are not in an exploitative dynamic with a third party. Throughout the training, the messaging is that individuals who are trading sex are victims and should not be arrested. As was reported earlier in this chapter, though, in the first year after the passage of Proposition 35, California reported 205 prostitution arrests of minors. It is clear that a victim-centered approach has not been fully implemented. At its essence, the training is a great example of "rescue porn." Such representations of this complex issue reduce it to situations where young cisgender women are provocatively dressed and are being exploited by a person of color until police officers come in and save them. The training conflates all forms of sex trades with trafficking and makes the unsubstantiated claim that most people trading sex have a pimp and that most were first exploited as minors (Bullard and Wygal 2014). The harms that can result from trainings such as this are significant.

Defining these young people's involvement in trading sex as criminal is "an extreme form of stigma and may alter [their] identification" (Schur 1965). Case managers share that the young people they work with, especially those with histories of prostitution arrests, report feeling as if they are different from "normal" people. The internalized stigma some of these young people experience is represented in the following statement a young cisgender woman made to her case manager: "I'm a ho, and I'm going to always be a ho, and I'm going to die a ho" (qtd. in C. Roberts, personal communication, March 9, 2011). The argument presented by the legal approach is that the only way to mandate these young people to services is to arrest them—that even if they are viewed as victims, they need to be funneled through the juvenile justice system to link them to care.

Although agreeing that part of the problem is how to connect youth to needed services, others have suggested that the child welfare system, as opposed to the juvenile justice system, is better equipped to deal with these young people (Brittle 2008) because it is already mandated to work with marginalized and vulnerable youth.[16] Illinois was the first state to test this theory by decriminalizing minors' involvement in trading sex by transferring their jurisdiction from the juvenile justice system to child welfare. Although the child welfare system may be preferable to juvenile justice, it is not without its flaws. A large proportion of these young people are already involved in the child welfare system. For example, 35 percent of the clients at STOP-IT in Chicago were in the system at the time I was doing research for this project. Those who age out of the foster-care system are doing so without the fundamental skills required to succeed in life, and one in four foster youth will be incarcerated within the first two years of exiting the system (Brittle 2008). As Minh Dang reflected, "Throwing them into child welfare is not going to do it; child welfare has already failed so many of these children" (personal communication, January 16, 2014). It is, of course, preferable that these young people not be arrested for prostitution-related offenses. Yet because it is not clear whether the child welfare system will produce significantly different results for these young people, an evaluation of the Illinois DCFS's ability to identify and serve young people who trade sex is needed.

Although the SHA adopts the TVPA's notion that these young people are victims of a severe form of human trafficking, it is problematic that it does not adopt the age provision and instead is limited to youth younger than sixteen. The provision in the SHA that prevents young people who are sixteen or seventeen from being eligible for a PINS provision is indicative of the ways in which age and notions about individuals' ability to consent factor into determinations of victimhood. Thus, some young people are victims who are eligible for PINS proceedings, but others are treated as criminals. Similarly, the exclusion of youth who have prior arrests for prostitution crimes is shortsighted. It fails to recognize the cyclical nature of this type of activity and young people's view of trading sex as a solution, maybe their only solution, to real problems. Those who are eligible for a PINS provision are still classified as status offenders (a juvenile who is charged with or adjudicated for conduct that legally would not be an offense if committed by an adult), which is stigmatizing and conveys the message that he or she did something wrong.

Under the SHA, one of the intents of moving the adjudication of juvenile prostitution from delinquency proceedings to PINS proceedings is to link young people to a continuum of services. However, the SHA's PINS provision is an unfunded mandate (Schwartz 2009), so the act does not guarantee the availability of needed services. The absence of funding coupled with the lack of secure housing for these young people calls into question the act's potential for success. The importance of connecting young people to services such as physical, mental, and sexual health care, housing, education, and employment opportunities cannot be overemphasized. Including New York, eleven other states have safe-harbor legislation. According to Lauren Jekowsky, an associate at the Human Trafficking Center, all safe-harbor legislation has "proven to be largely ineffective in most cases due to their incompleteness, poor implementation, and lack of resources and [so] need to be strengthened" (2014).

Considering the amount of monetary resources devoted to this issue, victim identification is low. Suggestions have been made that to increase victim identification, training efforts and anti-trafficking task forces need to be expanded (U.S. Department of State 2010). In fiscal years 2009 and 2010, the same period in which recommendations were made for task force expansions, the U.S. government devoted approximately $42.5 million to address, combat, and further understand domestic trafficking. With 44 percent of that total, $18.7 million, dedicated to training and task forces, it is not apparent how more task forces will result in more young people being identified.

Since 2003, the U.S. Office for Victims of Crime and the U.S. Bureau of Justice Administration have funded forty-two anti-trafficking task forces, inclusive of task forces in California, Illinois, and New York. Each task force comprises federal, state, and local law enforcement investigators and prosecutors, labor enforcement, and one victim-service nongovernmental organization (U.S. Department of State 2010). A review of these forty-two federally funded task forces found that less than half of them could be classified as having accumulated high-quality data (Banks and Kyckelhahn 2011). An article in *SF Public Press* also highlights some troubling aspects of these task forces (Winshell 2012). In 2007, a California state task force made recommendations for how the state could better respond to and prevent human trafficking. No mechanisms were put in place to monitor progress on the recommendations, however, and shortly thereafter the task force disbanded. Since then, nine regional task forces have formed throughout California. They receive no clear guidance from the state. Their efforts are supported largely by federal grants, yet although the grants indicate that the task forces' goals are to decrease the demand for human trafficking and to increase the number of individuals arrested for trafficking, they do not indicate deadlines for meeting these goals or clarify who should be arrested and who should not be. For instance, the San Francisco Police Department received permission to use some of its federal task force money to arrest adults who trade sex.

The Bureau of Justice has since applied more stringent standards to these task force grants. It remains to be seen if these new guidelines have had any effect. However, if the past experiences of the task forces in California are representative of other task forces, dedicating more money to them is not the solution. To date, no evaluation of such task forces has occurred (Institute of Medicine and the National Research Council 2013). Before more money is devoted to expanding task forces, a systematic evaluation of the current task forces' effectiveness needs to be conducted. Speaking at the annual Freedom Network Conference in 2014, Kristina Rose, deputy director of the Office for Victims of Crimes, expressed this same sentiment: "What OVC has decided is to use this year as a planning year. We want to take a deep dive and look at the victims' services and law enforcement pieces of this model. There is no evidence, scientific evidence, yet to show that this model is effective. . . . So we are going to be doing a very intensive assessment of the model."

Vacatur laws offer young people who have been convicted of prostitution-related offenses the important ability to have their records erased. Curiously, however, no affirmative defense exists in New York whereby young people who have been charged with prostitution can get their cases dismissed based on the fact that they are considered trafficking victims (Baskin 2014b). Kate Mogulesco, supervising attorney for the Trafficking Victims Advocacy Project at the Legal Aid Society, shared what happened when she tried to evoke an affirmative motion:

> We actually raised an affirmative motion to dismiss in Bronx Criminal Court a couple years ago the fact that our client was a trafficking victim. It was a motion to dismiss in the interest of justice and we cited the fact that she was 17 at the time she was arrested and that she actually gave very, very specific information about the people that were trafficking her but would not participate in a grand jury investigation. The Bronx DA's office, they opposed the motion[,] saying if she's a victim of trafficking let her vacate her convictions after but there's no remedy now. (2014)

Sixteen states, including New York and Illinois, have vacatur remedies. Although the specifics of the law vary state by state, none of them offers the ability to raise an affirmative motion.

Vacatur laws have some additional limitations. Many young people who trade sex are also engaged in other criminalized behavior. Unfortunately, many vacating laws are only for prostitution-related crimes. However, the Uniform Law Commission's version of vacating convictions allows for the vacation of prostitution-related offenses as well as of any nonviolent offenses that were the result of being a victim of any type of trafficking. This law, according to Sienna Baskin, codirector of the Sex Workers Project at the Urban Justice Center, "shows you what's possible and the limitations of some of the state laws" (2014b).

Despite their limitations, vacatur laws are a positive introduction to local anti-trafficking legislation. Any reduction in a young person's rap sheet is a move in the right direction. Erasing prostitution-related convictions provides the "opportunity [for] going forward so that [the] person does not have to explain these convictions in the future or be denied work opportunities or other opportunities because of their record" (Baskin 2014b). Furthermore, providing people the opportunity to come back in to criminal court, a space where they were previously convicted as criminals, and reclaim that space as a person with rights and dignity has proven to be a "powerful and meaningful experience for them" (Mogulesco 2014).

The United States currently does not have a federal-level vacatur law for minors involved in the sex trades. What this means is that if a young person is convicted in a federal case, a vacatur remedy is not available to that person. To ensure consistency across the states, to recognize the ways in which young people are often transient and will have cases in multiple states, and to offer assistance to those convicted at the federal level, the United States needs to enact a federal vacatur remedy.

7

MACROSYSTEM CHALLENGES

THE IMPACT OF POLICIES AND CULTURE

Several key macrosystem issues affect case managers' ability to work with young people who trade sex. Program staff face the seemingly insurmountable barriers of poverty, homelessness, and limited options. Current policies emphasize the importance of connecting these young people to a continuum of services. However, the lack of coordination among service providers is troubling. As described in chapter 5, youth who request mental health services are sometimes unable to receive them because their guardians or child welfare workers do not sign the necessary consent forms. This situation is avoidable. Policies need to be amended so that guardians can provide verbal rather than written consent and so that young people who have reached adolescence are able to request and receive services such as housing and health care on their own. An assessment is also needed to determine the best way in which youth can access emergency food stamps that does not require them to prove parental or guardian negligence. To treat all young people, regardless of whether they are one or seventeen, as needing the same types of protection ignores the ways in which most youth become significantly more independent as they age.

This chapter explores how the political and cultural contexts limit the range of options available to young people and introduces challenges for case managers. The absence or in some cases the inaccessibility of housing and viable employment options create further vulnerabilities for these youth. Likewise, homophobia and transphobia effectively limit the range of supportive options available to them. The social dynamics of some of the neighborhoods where they live can also inhibit their ability to choose alternative life courses. Finally, this chapter also describes the ways in which the dominant narrative about domestic minor sex trafficking creates idealized expectations about who these young people are, contributes to preconceived notions about their service needs, and essentially pathologizes them.

HOUSING NEEDS

One of the needs most difficult to address for these young people is housing. In both urban and rural communities, housing options range from scarce to nonexistent. Fiona Mason, clinical supervisor for Safe Horizon's anti-trafficking program, explains that "youth in urban areas with limited resources are often struggling to piece together support, on waiting lists for resources, or in competition for resources. In many rural areas youth survive without the existence of support structures and often in isolation from others who have had similar experiences. Unfortunately there are no magical solutions to these problems" (2013).

Eligibility requirements to obtain certain types of housing also prove to be an insurmountable barrier for some young people. To be eligible for supportive housing, someone needs a documented history of years of homelessness. In some situations, the odds of accessing housing can improve if the person has some type of mental health or substance-use diagnosis. What this means is that the lives of many of these young people "would have to get a lot worse . . . to have a chance" of securing supportive housing (J. Westmacott, personal communication, May 22, 2012). In other situations, though, exclusion criteria prohibit young people who have a severe mental health issue or current substance use issues from getting housing (Clawson and Gace 2007).

Even if ample housing were available for young people, because they all are younger than eighteen and most seemingly want to avoid child welfare involvement, case managers are limited in their ability to successfully link them to housing. Describing the situation of a seventeen-year-old cisgender woman with a baby, one case manager stated,

> So we've been working with her to try to find a long-term housing, [a] more stable kind of situation. It's hard because almost every single mother–child program, the youngest they go is eighteen years old. . . . If she was closer to her eighteenth birthday, she would have a lot more options and resources.

[N]ot that there's enough resources for eighteen-year-olds, young mothers, but . . . there's almost nothing available to a seventeen-year-old outside of [child welfare], which she wants to avoid because she's had a history with them before; she is not a fan of their services, and she feels confident that they would just take her child away from her if they put her into care, and she doesn't want that. (J. Westmacott, personal communication, May 21, 2012)

The combination of age and avoidance of child welfare essentially eliminates long-term housing options for these young people.

An additional challenge in securing housing for young people is that shelters rarely recognize these youth's increasing autonomy or intimate relationships. One young cisgender woman wanted help securing housing so she would no longer be homeless and on the street. Because it was important for her to stay with her boyfriend, her options became nonexistent. Her case manager explained: "None of the options in the city are really going to give them that. And part of that is ageism. People don't recognize that young people can have significant and important relationships, and part of that is just limited options. And then part of it also is that she's under eighteen, and so all of these barriers are in her path" (J. Skelton, personal communication, November 8, 2011).

In cases where young people are in legal domestic partnerships, the housing options available to them frequently only allow visitations, not cohabitation. In one situation, a young cisgender woman was in a domestic partnership, and case managers worked to help her get an independent-living situation through the city system. However, they were not sure if she would ultimately take the housing because "her domestic partner can't be in the space with her except for visiting. Like, overnight visitations are fine, but essentially the city system hasn't designed ways for poor people with mental health conditions and/or former foster care history to have families at any juncture. Somehow it's assumed that if you are in need of any support, you couldn't possibly also have a family" (M. Vilson, personal communication, May 21, 2012). Because these youth are younger than eighteen, want to avoid child welfare, and want to live with their intimate partners, they have limited to no housing options available to them.

Seeing how homelessness creates a need to engage in sex trades, housing options are desperately needed for young people. Although this need is widely acknowledged, there is a chronic shortage of beds available for youth. If we look at the ratio of shelter beds to young people who need them, the absence of housing becomes even more apparent. California has approximately one thousand shelter beds for the more than two hundred thousand homeless young people (California Homeless Youth Project, 2011). Jack Skelton, the housing coordinator for Streetwork in New York City, explains, "The problem is that of the 3,800 homeless youth in the city on any given night that are on the street, there are only 207 available beds" (personal communication, November 8, 2011).

Even though housing is widely recognized as a need for this group of youth, money is not specifically earmarked in policies for its provision. The TVPRA of 2008 maintained the provision set forth in the TVPRA of 2005 to support shelters. This provision never received funding (Kotrla 2010); however, the TVPRA of 2013 (sec. 202) created twelve-month block grants of $1,500,000 to $2,000,000 to be awarded to up to six qualified nongovernmental organizations that work with young people who trade sex. Although this is a step in the right direction, it remains to be seen how much of the money will be used for housing services.[1] Likewise, the use of the term *qualified* may be problematic. As Yvonne Zimmerman explains, not all organizations doing great work identify as anti-trafficking organizations:

When I look at organizations that are doing what I would consider anti-trafficking work that I respect, they aren't framing it as anti-trafficking work per se, but are looking to address safe and affordable housing, how to lower instances of violence at the hands of police officers, alternative economic development, working with queer youth. Those are the kind of things that get less press, because we've been having a housing crisis in the US for how long now? But that's where we actually get some traction on the micro things that make people vulnerable to trafficking. (qtd. in Campano 2013)

Some of the anti-trafficking funding that is dedicated to the needs of domestic minors must be earmarked for housing and for agencies that work with this population but do not frame their work as anti-trafficking. Recognizing young people's range of developmental needs, shelters need to create ways for them to maintain levels of autonomy (Williams 2010).

The Runaway and Homeless Youth Act (Title III of the Juvenile Justice and Delinquency Prevention Act) of 1974 established houses for runaways throughout the country to shelter youth and provide crisis interventions.[2] With homeless and runaway youth overrepresented among young people involved in sex trades, this act was an important contribution to their service needs, but it is limited in its impact.[3] It is estimated that no more than 6 percent of homeless and runaway youth receive shelter in federally funded programs (Loken 1986). The small number of homeless and runaway young people housed in shelters can be attributed to one provision of this act: shelters that receive federal funding are required to report the young person's whereabouts to his or her parent or guardian within seventy-two hours of his or her arrival at the shelter. In general, young people have valid reasons for leaving their homes or child welfare placements. For young people who do not want their whereabouts to be known, these shelters are not a resource. Because young people who are runaways and homeless often do not utilize these more traditional programs (Greene, Ennett, and Ringwalt 1999), drop-in centers and outreach programs need to be increased to reach them. Similarly, because many young people eschew housing options in order to avoid child welfare, innovative ideas such as having drop-in programs that operate twenty-four hours a day may offer them an alternative to trading sex for a place to sleep. The inability to access shelters is a major barrier for young people who want to stop trading sex (Pierce 2012). Johannah Westmacott, a case manager in New York, explained, "If they have a safe, age-appropriate place to sleep, they don't trade sex for a place to sleep" (personal communication, November 7, 2011).

EMPLOYMENT NEEDS

Viable employment opportunities are one of the other most difficult to meet needs for this group of young people, largely because these youth have minimal to no previous legal work experience and have not graduated high school or obtained a GED. A case manager in New York described the difficulties of trying to help a young man find work when he would be competing with people who have more qualifications: "He's like, 'Can you help me find [a job]?' and it's like we would love to do that, [but] there are people with master's degrees that can't find entry level work right now, you know, and he doesn't even have a high school diploma yet. He's in school and wants to get it, but how is he going to compete? He has no work experience, no legal work experience" (J. Westmacott, personal communication, March 23, 2011).

The issue of obtaining employment is compounded by the reality that many of these young people have the experience of making a seemingly large amount of money in a short amount of time through trading sex. As a consequence, some of the entry-level jobs that might be available do not offer what they consider to be a living wage. Case managers reported that some young people told them, " 'I've worked for this amount, and I don't want to go down [work for less]' " (S. Larrea, personal communication, October 18, 2011). Regarding her work with a young cisgender woman, Johannah Westmacott explained that "she wants a job that she could live off of. She doesn't want to go work at McDonald's. . . . I mean, nobody wants to work at McDonald's, but you can't live off of that anyway so there's not much motivation" (personal communication, November 7, 2011). A Department of Youth and Family Services worker in New Jersey acknowledged, "What can you do? They would rather make $100 for a trick than working at Subway for $7.25 an hour. It's their choice. I can't really blame them" (qtd. in Marcus and Curtis 2013, 7).

With limited to no options for legal employment, young people consider reengaging in sex trades. When one young cisgender woman's boyfriend, who had been her sole provider, was incarcerated, she had no way to take care of herself financially and tried to find a job. Without previous work experience and without a diploma, "she was not successful in finding other ways to support herself and was very stressed out about the fact that she saw this as an inevitability that she would have to go back and do things she didn't want to do because she didn't feel like she had any other options" (J. Westmacott, personal communication, November 7, 2011).

In another case, a young cisgender woman had transitioned away from trading sex and was living with her mother. Even though her mother was receiving financial benefits, she was not financially supporting her daughter. The young woman's case manager was working with her to find a job, and when that did not materialize, the young woman had no other option but to "fall back into the lifestyle" (N. Woodcox, personal communication, April 25, 2012).

Viable employment options are desperately needed for these young people. The modernization of work has delayed young people's entry into the labor force (Moffitt 1993), and most youth are not legally allowed to work until they are sixteen. Even once they reach the legal age, many lack the skills and qualifications necessary to get a job. The difficulty of finding employment, coupled with the low wages available, is often identified as a deterrent for leaving sex trades. Innovative approaches to helping young people fulfill their economic needs are required. In New York City, Streetwise & Safe (SAS), a peer-run internship program for LGBTQ youth of color is an example of one such approach. SAS conducts "know your rights" workshops that focus on ways youth can increase their safety and reduce the harms of interactions with police officers. The program also creates opportunities for youth to identify a policy issue that is relevant to their lived experiences and acquire the necessary skills to speak out on their own behalf and work collectively to address their rights. Johannah Westmacott at the Streetwork Project explained the positive role this internship played for one of her clients:

[She is] getting paid to do work, and so it's a really nice model because not only are they showing up because they're getting paid, . . . but the fact that they're getting paid speaks directly to her [sense of her] worthlessness, her unintelligence, how she can't do anything but sex work. [The internship is] the exact opposite of all those things, where someone is valuing her; they are depending on her being there and doing these other things like building up a community that would speak to other young people in her situation. [S]he does get a lot out of it, and I don't think she's just going for the money, but I think that paying her for her time is part of what speaks to her worth in being there. (personal communication, March 23, 2011)

In addition to increasing the number of paid internship programs available to youth, developing microenterprise projects that target young people who are engaged in sex trades may provide them with other employment opportunities (Hodge 2008).

HOMOPHOBIA AND TRANSPHOBIA

The effects of homophobia and transphobia compromise case managers' ability to work effectively with young people who trade sex. Both of these forms of structural violence effectively push some youth out of their homes and onto the streets, where they turn to sex trades to support themselves. A case manager in Chicago shared the perspective of an adoptive mother who did not accept her transgender daughter: " 'You are just one person, and my family is this big enormous family, and I'd rather lose just one person than lose my entire family over you.' So that was the bottom line at the end of the day; that's what it was: 'I'm not going to lose my entire family over you; it's not worth it. I love you so much, but I just cannot lose everyone over you.' So that's what it was" (A. Velasquez, personal communication, October 31, 2011). Once youth are out on the streets, case managers are faced with the challenge of finding appropriate housing options for them.

Linking young LGBTQ people to mental health services is also complicated by the ways in which homophobia and transphobia have influenced some mental health providers to consider individuals' gender or sexual identity to be the presenting problem. Instances in which young transgender women have been placed involuntarily in psychiatric units (Iman et al. 2009) or in which young people have suffered through conversion therapies (Croce 2014) foster a real fear about mental health services among LGBTQ youth. Work needs to take place to figure out how best to link LGBTQ young people to supportive mental health services.

LGBTQ youth also face harassment in their schools and on the street. A case manager in New York shared the story of a young transgender woman attending a cosmetology school who faced hostility from the students, staff, and administration. "She even described one incident where the principal of the school under his breath called her a faggot. They don't, the school does not approve of how she dresses. [The principal] has totally had the conversation with her around, like, 'You're kind of bringing this on yourself,' you know. 'We can't help you because you're obviously instigating these things by dressing in female clothing' " (J. Westmacott, personal communication, May 22, 2012).

Unfortunately, few resources and services exist for transgender youth. In the case of the young woman who was committed to becoming a cosmetologist, she decided to stay at the school despite the harassment because there were no other cosmetology schools in the city where she lived. All young people deserve the right to safety at school. When this safety is compromised, many drop out and face the challenge of obtaining employment without a high school degree or GED.

In addition to the challenge of finding supportive school environments for transgender youth in some cities, no appropriate group-home options exist for young transgender people in some cities. Some shelters will not house transgender youth at all. Magalie Lerman, codirector of Prax(us), explains the situation in Denver, Colorado: "Denver does not have that many trans-inclusive services, especially in terms of survivor specific transitional housing programs. I have this experience of working with people and sometimes I'll be working all day and then at 11 o'clock at night I'll go meet them somewhere and we would call 24 hour hotlines all night long. We would start by asking them about their program. Then a week later we would start by asking, 'Hey, do you take transwomen? No. Okay, bye.' And that's a lot of what our experience is like" (2014). Among shelters and housing placements that will work with transgender youth, they oftentimes place young people based on their biological sex, so young transgender women find themselves put in homes with cisgender young men. These placements leave them vulnerable to verbal, physical, and sexual assaults by staff and peers alike.

To address young people's concern about safety and increase the likelihood that transgender youth will access housing options, programs must incorporate the needs of transgender youth into their protocols. These protocols would allow for assignment of placements and housing accommodations to be based on a person's self-reported gender identity and would work toward having private accommodations available. In addition, matching youth with LGBTQ supportive program staff and foster parents is critical (Burwick et al. 2014). Work needs to be done to ensure the safety of and appropriate service delivery for transgender youth. Even when appropriate services do exist for transgender youth, their safety is sometimes compromised when they travel to get to these services. A case manager described the experiences of one young transwoman who was coming to a program for an intake: "Unfortunately, on her way in the door somebody outside the program started like harassing her, calling her like homophobic and transphobic slurs and even making gun noises at her. And so her entry into the program, like on her way there, you know, she had, I mean, she was bashed, verbally bashed, and then, so I was meeting with her to do her intake, and she was just so shaken up by that; she didn't feel safe to come back to that neighborhood" (J. Westmacott, personal communication, May 22, 2012).

NEIGHBORHOOD FACTORS

The impact of neighborhoods plays out in other ways for young people and their case managers. Neighborhoods characterized by violence, drug use, and street economies inhibit some of these young people's ability to choose alternative paths for themselves. Reminiscent of Edwin Sutherland's (1934) theory of differential association, case managers explain how their clients' interactions with people in their neighborhoods sometimes push them to maintain behaviors the case managers consider problematic. When some young people try not to engage in sex trades, men in their neighborhoods who know that they used to be involved in "the life" will approach them and "try to negotiate a price" for sex" (N. Yoon, personal communication, April 24, 2012). Case managers describe how in some of these neighborhoods nearly everyone has a history of incarceration and substance use and assert that it is just a matter of time before their clients revert to behaviors they are trying to leave behind. As one case manager put it, "You can't have a person trying to overcome crack surrounded by current crack users" (N. Woodcox, personal communication, April 25, 2012). Because of probation requirements, some young people are legally required to stay in the very neighborhoods where they experienced violence and exploitation by traffickers and law enforcement officials (R. Richardson 2014). It is clear that placing young people back in these communities does not offer them the support they need to thrive.

THE NARRATIVE OF DOMESTIC MINOR SEX TRAFFICKING

The dominant narrative of a young cisgender girl forced to trade sex also poses challenges for case managers when it results in service providers approaching their work with this group of young people in a romanticized way. Nicole Woodcox, case manager for STOP-IT, described how this approach played out for a young cisgender woman she worked with: "[Service providers] were just expecting something different. They expected to have this huge, grand rescue story where it's like, 'Yea! Thank you for helping me! You rescued me!' [and they] just romanticize[d] it. But instead they got someone who was like, 'No, I don't want to do that' . . . 'I don't feel like doing that,' and it just took them off guard. [They were] like, 'Why is she saying she doesn't want to do this? Why is she not happy?' So they just was expecting the whole romantic story, I guess" (personal communication, April 25, 2012). This comment illustrates how the dominant narrative about domestic minor victims of human trafficking can confound service providers' attempts to work with this population. Youth who do not conform to these preconceived notions find that their needs and perspectives are silenced or ignored. Penelope Saunders, coordinator of the Best Practices Policy Project, addressed how nonconforming youth are effectively excluded from services: "Youth who no longer look or act like small, frightened children but wish to speak out about their own lives and construct their own futures, which may not include marriage, the nuclear family, and sober middle-class values are not fully invited into the 'participatory framework'" (2005, 180).

Narratives that construct youth as passive and trapped obscure their more complicated reality. They position youth as needing rescuing and fail to recognize young people's agency and self-determination (Barry 1979; Gibbons, Lichtenberg, and van Beusekom 1994). This positioning is best described as "victimism," a framework wherein the person is viewed as a victim, not a "living, changing, growing" person (Barry 1979, 45). Not only are youth rendered "passive receptacles and mute sufferers who must be saved" (Agustín 2007, 39), but those in the helping profession are positioned as saviors. When service providers interact with a young person whose lived experience contradicts this prioritized narrative, the complexity of the situation seemingly confounds the simplistic attempts to "rescue" him or her.

Positioning these young people as victims not only results in idealized expectations among service providers but also alienates young people and prevents them from wanting to access services. If the services are offered as "victim services," young people will rarely self-select to use these them because they do not think of themselves as victims. Likewise, young people largely resent social service providers' attempts to "rescue" them because such attempts ignore the ways in which their resourcefulness and resilience have kept them alive (Williams 2010). In their work with young people in New York City, Anthony Marcus and Ric Curtis found that the among those they interviewed, the trafficking "narrative that identifies

their biggest problems as being too young to consent to sex and living under the shadow of pimp coercion appeared absurd, insulting and too far
from reality to make them want to engage such social services" (2013, 8).
Indeed, as Lucy Berliner, director of the University of Washington's Harborview Center for Sexual Assault and Traumatic Stress, suggests, the
pimp-focused approach misses the reality that most of these young people
do not have someone forcing them to trade sex (cited in Hess 2014).

An additional complication associated with the dominant trafficking narrative is that it presents the misinformed claim that only cisgender young
women are involved in trading sex. Even more troubling is the fact that the
narrative ultimately positions cisgender boys as perpetrators or perpetrators-to-be. An increasing trend is to offer curriculum in middle and high
schools that seeks to deter young men from "becoming pimps" (Tucker
2013) and to educate them "about the harms of prostitution" (Chicago Alliance Against Sexual Exploitation 2010). As a consequence, some programs
are unwilling to work with cisgender boys (Friedman 2013) or are willing to
work with them only if they are training them not to be perpetrators (Croce
2014). At the same time, this training tells young cisgender women that they
"are one step away from being a victim" (M. Dang, personal communication,
January 16, 2014). Absent from this model is an acknowledgment of the ways
in which adults have created situations and systems that make young people
more vulnerable. As a consequence, "the way we have thought about and
labeled victims has hindered the possibility of acknowledging the pervasive-
ness of abuse on a political level" (Lamb 1999, 109). The model perpetuates
the overly simplistic idea that if we simply warn young cisgender girls not
to let this happen to them and educate young cisgender boys not to be perpetrators, then we will be able to eradicate young people's involvement in
trading sex.

When asked to identify their needs, young people most often cite employment and housing (Curtis et al. 2008), yet these two services seem to be
the ones missing from the local response efforts. Conversely, when service
providers are asked to identify the most needed service among young people who trade sex, they routinely answer that it is mental health care. This
orientation positions young people who trade sex as being sick in their

mind. By pathologizing the individual, it offers little explanation about the push-and-pull factors that exist outside of individuals and are associated with their involvement trading sex, and it provides the simplistic solution of mental health treatment. Thomas Szasz (2001) argues that a disease and a problem are two different things and that "pharmacracy" is the process whereby medicine, especially psychiatry, is used as a method of social control. The labeling of all young people who trade sex as needing mental health services renders the issue apolitical (Lamb 1999) and situates trading sex as a mental health problem as opposed to a social problem. According to this view, the solution to the problem is within the individual, and it is the individual who needs to change and not society; as a result, the ways in which involvement in sex trades is an adaptation to a social situation is all but ignored (Conrad and Schneider 1980). As Minh Dang explains this approach, "Oftentimes [the recommended solution is] go to therapy and heal yourself. We need to do a lot more than that to heal ourselves" (2014). When responses to this issue rely on the opinions of experts such as service providers, law enforcement officials, and activists about these young people's service needs, it is questionable whether services are being offered that youth want to receive.

To ensure relevancy and buy-in, these young people need to be included in all aspects of services, from planning to implementation. An empowerment model recognizes that young people who trade sex are capable of making their own decisions and defining what success means for them. This remains true even if young people's actions and decisions contradict what service providers believe to be the best course of action for them (Iman et al. 2009). Yvonne Zimmerman, assistant professor of Christian ethics at the Methodist Theological School in Ohio, states, "I remain skeptical about anti-trafficking practices, or practices of freedom, that implicitly or explicitly presume that persons who have experienced trafficking necessarily need others to imagine freedom for them, on their behalf" (2013, 181). Programs that do not allow young people to self-identify their needs simply maintain social control over them and perpetuate the ways in which society denies them power and control. Young people who trade sex routinely have their needs disregarded. One of the most powerful things programs can do is to create spaces and opportunities for these youth themselves to make decisions about program development and implementation and to provide regular feedback so that meaningful change can be made when needed (Croce 2014). Providing opportunities for peer support and peer leadership acknowledges these young people's resilience and resourcefulness and provides them with the opportunity to own their power.

8

CONCLUSION

Young people who trade sex rarely think of themselves as victims (Cates 1989; Curtis et al. 2008; Schwartz 2009; Tiapula and Turkel 2008; Walker 2002; Williams 2009). They are instead constructing their own life course to the best of their ability, with their choices shaped by the opportunities and constraints of their circumstances (Elder 1998). For many, trading sex gives them a "sense of control and power" (C. Harris, personal communication, May 21, 2012). Although their choice to trade sex is made under the constraints of limited options, poverty, abuse, and neglect, they argue that calling them victims "robs them of autonomy" (Sherman 2012, 1608). Trading sex affords them the opportunity to leave abusive homes and provide for themselves. In situations where their families do not provide for them, it becomes a way to assert their independence and get their needs met. In response to the ways in which their access to power has been limited through laws that influence their ability to work in legitimate jobs and enter into contracts, as well as by negligent or abusive parents and guardians, these youth are trying to regain power and control.

For the majority of these young people, a third party facilitates or benefits from their sex trades. Although facilitating or benefitting financially or both constitute the legal definition of pimping and pandering, it is rare for young people to think of these third parties as "pimps." Young people couple with third parties for a variety of reasons. These other individuals can be intimate partners who provide emotional support. Some are directly involved in arranging young people's sex trades. Others have no involvement but benefit financially. In cases where a young person's relationship with the person starts as an emotional one, over time it may become more contractual and controlling (Mukasey, Daley, and Hagy 2007). Youth who are not accepted by their biological or adopted families because of their gender or sexual identity or those who feel they are not loved within their families sometimes view third parties as surrogate family members. Ron Riggin, a retired Maryland state police sergeant, explained that "the pimps give the victims the attention and sense of belonging that vulnerable children desire" (qtd. in Pupovac 2013). Some third parties simply let the young person use their homes to work out of or connect youth with clients, and in return they receive a portion of the young person's earnings. For many youth, it is their friends and peers who teach them how to trade sex and connect with clients.

In general, young people identify their relationships with third parties as important. This is true whether the third party is their intimate partner or a surrogate family member or a friend. The arrangements they have with these people provide them with a sense of belonging and a sense of being loved and accepted. Alternatively, some young people are simply trying to get out of one abusive situation, be it at home or in child welfare placements, and are willing to couple with someone who may or may not be abusive as well (Marcus et al. 2014).

Some young people never choose to couple with a third party and instead find that as a continuation of the sexual abuse they experience from family members, those mothers, fathers, aunts, and uncles are now forcing them to sell sex (M. Dang, personal communication, January 16, 2014; Mitchell, Finkelhor, and Wolak 2010; O'Connell Davidson 1998; E. Sims, personal communication, July 31, 2014; Sims 2012). It is clear that people who act as third parties are not a homogenous group.

Even though in most states these young people have not reached the legal age of consent for sex, they are still arrested for a sexual encounter that under other laws would be classified as rape or statutory rape. This contradictory system of regulations places them in the troubling position of being viewed as both an exploited youth and an individual granted total agency and held to adult standards. Although young people of various ages are arrested for prostitution offenses, the finding that those who appear frightened, are cisgender women, and are younger than sixteen are more likely to be considered victims suggests that victim status is based on social concepts about childhood and innocence.

The federal definition put forth through the TVPA classifies this group of young people as victims who should not be arrested for prostitution-related offenses and should not be placed in juvenile detention facilities. To ensure that youth are not arrested for prostitution-related offenses, their involvement in prostitution needs to be decriminalized. The American Bar Association's Child Trafficking Policy is in agreement with the TVPA that it should be prohibited to arrest or charge young people "with the crimes of prostitution, solicitation, or loitering as well as other offenses, including status offenses that are incident to their trafficking situation" (American Bar Association 2011). Judge Fernando Camacho, administrative judge for criminal matters in Queens County, New York, started a court that works with young people who have been charged with prostitution-related offenses. His opinion is that "jail is not the right place for these young people. A young person is presumed to be not competent to consent under certain statutory sex offenses, yet the same young person who is not even capable of consenting is now going to be prosecuted as an adult for engaging in prostitution and prostitution-related offenses. And that never made any sense. That's just silly" (in Schweig 2012).

It is logically inconsistent to say that young people are not able to consent to sex but then to criminalize them for trading sex. To address the tension that currently exists between viewing them as victims and treating them as criminals, all states need to incorporate a minimum age into their laws whereby no one younger than eighteen can be charged for prostitution-related offenses. In fact, the International Committee on the Rights of the Child criticized the U.S. government in 2013 for continuing to criminalize people younger than eighteen who trade sex (Phillips et al. 2014). Section 1243 of the TVPRA of 2013 offers the elements of a model state statute. This model includes not charging or prosecuting young people for prostitution offenses; not requiring them to prove force, fraud, or coercion;[1] and requiring the referral to appropriate services inclusive of community-based organizations. Decriminalization is the only way to ensure that young people are not arrested or detained for prostitution-related offenses.

In addition to aligning state with federal law, decriminalizing young people's involvement in trading sex also directly addresses the ways in which criminal convictions create lifelong barriers to obtaining housing, employment, financial aid for education, and other social welfare benefits—the very things that young people need to be able to transition away from trading sex. Any time a young person has a criminal conviction, their vulnerabilities increase, and the options available for them shrink dramatically. These collateral consequences, of course, limit case managers' ability to connect their clients to services and other forms of support. Once convicted, young people face barriers to employment, housing, benefits, and educational goals, which effectively compromises their ability to create a new life course. Indeed, people with convictions sometimes find that their only option to make money is to continue to engage in criminalized activities such as trading sex (Lerman 2014; Phillips et al. 2014). Robin Richardson, Equal Justice Fellow at the Urban Justice Center's Sex Workers Project, offers her perspective on the vulnerability created by convictions: "It's my personal belief that to the extent that a criminal record forces somebody to stay in prostitution, the state has at least committed the actus reus [the act that cause the crime] of trafficking. They may not have committed the mens rea [criminal intent], but they are at least reckless. A criminal conviction for prostitution makes people more vulnerable to being trafficked by other people" (2014). Ultimately, convictions are enduring barriers that place youth right back in the situations of vulnerability that resulted in their trading sex in the first place.

Because of the incentive to prosecute, young people are being tried and convicted as co-conspirators to their sex trades involvement. This treatment is morally reprehensible, brands young people as sex offenders for life, and limits them to a life without options because of that label. An additional problem relates to how many young people help coordinate other young people's sex trades. Common harm reduction techniques on the street such as working in pairs, using condoms, and providing information about potential clients are criminalized and can result in young people being charged as traffickers (Brennan 2014; Dorsey 2013; McLemore 2012; Medina 2014). The TVPRA of 2003 expanded the predicate acts that can be prosecuted under the Racketeer Influenced and Corrupt Organizations (RICO) Act of 1970 to include human trafficking. The TVPRA of 2008 added to the list of RICO offenses the provision of condoms manufactured outside of the state where the offense occurred. In the guise of being tough on crime and going after purported perpetrators, the current anti-trafficking laws ultimately criminalize young people's support systems and their fundamental right to health-promoting material such as condoms. Tamar R. Birkhead, associate professor of law and the director of Clinical Programs at the University of North Carolina, Chapel Hill, reflected on the problem of young people acting as recruiters: "Should these teenage recruiters also be criminally prosecuted and punished? What if the pimp is even younger than the prostituted child? Perhaps even more vexing, what ought to be done when a prostituted child recruits another child—her own peer—into the Life?" (2011, 1091–1092).

Recognizing the competing priorities of law enforcement and young people, the TVPRA of 2008 removed the provision that required young people to provide reasonable assistance in investigating and prosecuting their trafficker in order to be able to receive assistance and services. Suzanne Tomatore, co-chair of the Freedom Network, a national coalition of anti-human-trafficking service organizations, argues, "We all want to do the right thing, but I think it is important that the individual rights come first and [the victims] aren't pressured into cooperating with law enforcement" (qtd. in Pupovac 2013). Echoing this sentiment, Ambassador Luis CdeBaca in the U.S. State Department Office to Monitor and Combat Trafficking in Persons suggests that young people's needs and choices should be "as important as the needs of the state, the needs of prosecution, the needs of law enforcement" (qtd. in Kovtun 2013).

In an attempt to remove some of the negative impacts of being convicted of prostitution-related offenses even when legally considered a trafficking victim, several states have passed vacatur remedies. Most of these remedies apply only to prostitution-related offenses and fail to acknowledge the ways in which people engage in multiple criminalized activities surrounding their sex trades. Although it would be preferable to expunge all convictions related to young people's involvement in trading sex, as Kate Mogulesco, supervising attorney for the Trafficking Victims Advocacy Project at the Legal Aid Society, explains, "vacating any convictions helps our clients, especially our clients who are still facing arrest. If you're able to reduce their rap sheet by this much [holds up thumb to finger] that's a help to them" (2014). Indicative of the importance of having vacatur remedies, the Council of State Governments voted to include Kentucky Senate Bill 184 in their suggested state legislation volume for the year 2016 (J. Horne, personal communication, August 20, 2014).[2] Kentucky's vacatur remedy allows for the vacation of all nonviolent offenses that occurred while involved in trafficking situations, inclusive of young people who trade sex. All states need to enact vacatur remedies to ensure that young people's vulnerabilities are not enhanced by the very system that purports to protect them.

In addition to decriminalizing young people's involvement in trading sex, future work needs to examine the ways in which decriminalizing or legalizing adult prostitution may have an impact on young people's involvement in sex trades. It is possible that if a system for adults to procure sex were formalized through decriminalization or legalization, opportunistic clients would no longer have a need to purchase sex from young people. Similarly, removing criminal statutes against all individuals who sell and purchase sex may create an environment where they could report to law enforcement officials without fear of legal consequences any situations where people are being exploited in the sex industry.. In their report about effective legal remedies for trafficking victims, Suzannah Phillips and other attorneys at the International Women's Human Rights Clinic and City University of New York School of Law suggest that "individuals in the sex industry often have information about individuals forced into sex work and can report situations of exploitation and trafficking. Yet, fear of arrest or police harassment can pose a huge barrier to providing assistance for trafficked individuals" (2014, 23).

If nothing else, all people involved in trading sex—clients, third parties, and those who trade sex—regardless of age need to be guaranteed immunity if they choose to come forward to law enforcement and file reports when they are victims of crimes or when they want to report other crimes or abuses they have witnessed while engaged in trading sex. Granting young people immunity is clearly just the first step in acknowledging the ways in which law enforcement officials have become yet another exploiter in the lives of these young people. Among other things, a significant and meaningful investment in the restorative justice process is needed.

Looking beyond U.S. borders,[3] we find an example of what is possible when trading sex is not criminalized. In India, prostitution is legal, so people involved in the sex industry can work collectively to identify and address the social and structural factors that have negative impacts on them. In 1996, the Durbar Mahila Samanwaya Committee (DMSC), a collective of sixty-five thousand sex workers in West Bengal, decided that it wanted to work to address the issue of young people and coerced adults involved in sex work (Jana et al. 2013). As of 2011, the DMSC ran thirty-three self-regulatory boards in West Bengal, comprising ten to twelve members—six to seven sex workers and the rest representatives from the government, legal, social welfare, and health sectors.

To ensure that no youth or coerced adults are trading sex, the regulatory boards screen all newcomers to the red-light districts in West Bengal (DMSC 2013). In instances when it is determined that someone in the trade is younger than eighteen, either through self-report or analysis of a bone X-ray, the board decides a course of action with the young person. If returning home is not an option, often because of abusive conditions, the board arranges for alternative placements, such as short-stay homes and boarding schools. When appropriate, young people are also linked to vocational training or helped to find placements in other occupations (S. Jana, personal communication, February 11, 2014). It is important to note that not all the young people screened by the regulatory boards are appreciative of their efforts. Dr. Smarajit Jana, principal of the Sonagachi Research Training Institute, shared that some "express their anger . . . [and] see [the intervention as] oppressive and [an] infringement of their rights" (personal communication, February 11, 2014).

Some of the youth identified will never trade sex because of the DMSC regulatory boards' efforts, some will move to other districts where the regulatory boards do not operate, and others will wait until they are eighteen and then engage in sex work (S. Jana, personal communication, February 11, 2014). From 2001 to 2011, the regulatory boards identified 668 young people involved in trading sex, and since 1992 they have witnessed a 90 percent decline in the number of young people involved in sex work (Jana et al. 2013). Interestingly, from 2007 through 2009, the time period that data were reported, DMSC regulatory boards identified and assisted 259 young people, whereas the police identified only 90 (Jana et al. 2013). The approach utilized by the DMSC highlights the ways in which a community-led strategy rather than one driven by law enforcement provides the opportunity for more young people to be identified.

The United Nations has called for an increase in participatory interventions that address the social and structural factors that create, reinforce, and reproduce risk among young people who trade sex (Miller et al. 2011). Although some programs in the United States have placed young people who trade sex in positions of leadership, they are the exception rather than the rule. What is more common is programs perpetuating the same power dynamics that young people experience in exploitative situations: "People are getting *a*, *b*, *c*, and *d*. Usually shelter, food and a certain amount of love. They have to give *a*, *b*, *c*, and *d*. So they have to be that good client, in by 10 at night, and work all these groups. That can be very similar to the same things they are getting in an exploitative situation, which is shelter, food and conditional love, and the same things they have to do which is be loyal, be back to their exploiter by a certain time at night and make money, those power dynamics feel the same" (Lerman 2014).

To begin to move toward an empowerment, antioppression model of program development and service delivery, funders need to involve young people in the process from the beginning. These young people are resourceful and resilient, and they are the experts about their lives. They are capable of offering what they consider to be the solutions to their issues. Without their input and inclusion, service providers will continue to struggle when working with young people who trade sex. In fact, "a closer look suggests that what professes to be social welfare is often social control" of young people who frustrate systems by not playing by their rules (Sherman 2012, 1586). Programs need to be committed to creating opportunities for young people to develop and enhance their skills so they are able to take on additional leadership roles within and beyond the organization. Funding and delivering formal leadership programs for these young people are crucial.

Laws alone are not sufficient to prevent youth from trading sex. Young people also need social and economic power as well as the ability to have their choices about living situations, service needs, and sexuality respected. Unfortunately, because the United States is one of only three countries that has not ratified the United Nations Convention on the Rights of the Child,[4] it appears that we are not really interested in empowering our young people. Minh Dang recounted the following conversation she shared with a friend: "A friend of mine said this really beautifully. She identifies as a survivor of child abuse and trafficking and she said it's pretty telling that as a society we don't really value children's rights, we don't have universal children's rights because adult voters can vote away funding for education. Children have no say in that. Adults can literally say, 'We're not going to teach our kids, we're not going to give kids health care.' So how are we at all respecting children's rights?" (personal communication, January 16, 2014). If as a nation we ratify the Convention on the Rights of the Child, we would be obligated to listen to young people and take seriously their opinions. We also would be required to ensure that young people have access to health care, education, and social benefits.

If we truly care about our young people, we would recognize the ways in which many of our current laws and policies increase their vulnerability to trading sex and how none of the anti-trafficking laws address the root factors of trafficking. Young people trade sex when they need a place to stay and often eschew shelter options because they do not want child welfare involvement. Young people should be allowed to enter into binding contracts for property if they can provide sufficient proof that they are financially able to honor the contract. Recognizing the challenge for people younger than eighteen to make enough money to be able to prove financial ability, we also need to revisit the restrictions and guidelines that relate to shelters. Policies that require shelter staff to report the young person's presence to parents and guardians within a specified time period, typically seventy-two hours, effectively keep young people from entering shelters. The reporting provisions need to be eliminated to ensure all young people feel comfortable accessing shelter services. Young people have the right to access all forms of health care—mental, physical, and sexual. Laws that require parental or guardian consent prevent some young people from receiving these important services. Parental and guardian consent should not be required to access health care.

The framing of young people's involvement in trading sex as victimization through "domestic minor sex trafficking" has resulted in an increase in media attention, funding for services, and state and federal legislation. Although this shift from viewing youth as criminals to considering them victims of crimes began more than fourteen years ago, the unfortunate reality is we have not made much progress in truly addressing the root causes of this social issue. Rachel Lloyd, founder and chief executive of Girls Educational & Mentoring Service, offered her perspective on this issue in a piece she wrote for the *Huffington Post*: "In an effort to get people to care about this issue, we've been less than careful with the statistics and in an effort to get the media to cover this story we've often reduced it to the most basic elements. I've been guilty of this too. We've focused on quick fixes and good vs. evil responses that rarely address the true causes or empower the young people that we're serving" (2012).

Relying on this victim–villain narrative has prevented us from examining the structural factors and social forces that produce and maintain young people's vulnerability. Bree Pearsall, a human trafficking outreach advocate for the Bluegrass Rape Crisis Center in Lexington, Kentucky, acknowledged, "I don't think that we see people who are against eradicating human trafficking. . . . I think where the pushback is addressing some of those core vulnerability issues. . . . Why do we have children being prostituted on our streets? Those are the harder questions I think we have to ask ourselves as a community because we can really rally around eradication of slavery but it's those more really ground-level issues that I think are perpetuating the problem" (in Shaw 2010).

The "inaccurate and irresponsible" content of most descriptions of domestic minor sex trafficking has resulted in misinformed people supporting "policies and organizations that are ultimately counter-productive to the fight against human trafficking" (Turner 2014). It is our obligation to critically examine all current and proposed anti-trafficking legislation and assess whether it is directly helping or harming young people.

A more holistic and nuanced picture of youth who trade sex clearly demonstrates that campaigns focusing on ratcheting up penalties for third parties and clients will not in and of themselves result in young people leaving the sex industry. These young people have been forced to trade sex by parents and family members; they have been pushed out of or run away from home and are trying to survive; they are cisgender and transgender youth who are looking for emotional support and validation; they are in abusive relationships. Just as important as looking at what preceded their involvement, we also need to acknowledge what it takes for young people to stop trading sex. Many will stop on their own when their emotional, financial, and survival needs are provided for in other ways. When we pay attention to these diverse narratives and recognize the rarity in which youth are forced into trading sex by someone unknown to them, we realize that the root causes of young people's involvement in sex trades are not easily changed. Likewise, we see that the solution to this issue is not as simple as focusing efforts on "rescuing" youth and punishing "bad" people. Instead, attention needs to be directed at how the failure of social and cultural systems influences youth to trade sex in the first place. Speaking to this need to critically examine structural inequalities, Minh Dang suggests that "perhaps this is a good opportunity for anti-trafficking activists to say you can't fix trafficking without fixing inequalities in education, and racism, and poverty, and on and on and on. It's the perfect way to say, look, this is our messed up system coming to a head" (personal communication, January 16, 2014).

In the absence of an anti-oppression framework that addresses the systemic issues that create vulnerabilities—sexism, classism, racism, homophobia, transphobia, generational violence and abuse—we will never eradicate the social issue of young people trading sex. Young people need micro-, meso- and macrosystems that facilitate their holistic development. Without a functioning system to support them, young people find that to meet their needs, their best, only, or least-worst option is to trade sex.

Evoking the spirit of Pierre Bourdieu's notion of "*amor fati*, the choice of destiny, but a forced choice, produced by the conditions of existence which rule out all the alternatives as mere daydreams and leave no choice but the taste for the necessary" (1984, 178), a case manager in New York explained, "Yes, they're forced, but they're forced by the fact that there are no other options. . . . And there's some adults that take advantage of the situation, but . . . if we took those situations away it would impact the amount of young people who are vulnerable to those type of predatory adults. . . . [I]t's so frustrating that people are trying to find this complicated answer" (J. Westmacott, personal communication, November 7, 2011).

If young people's basic human rights are met, if they have stable and safe housing, employment or another source of income, health care, access to education and welfare benefits, and supportive networks (familial or social), those who really do not want to be trading sex will have other options.

APPENDIX A

STUDY SITE INFORMATION

The three programs that provided me with client data and case history narratives were funded by the federal Office for Victims of Crime (OVC) to provide comprehensive services to domestic minor victims of human trafficking. This appendix provides a brief description of each program.

CALIFORNIA: STANDING AGAINST GLOBAL EXPLOITATION PROJECT, INC.

The Standing Against Global Exploitation (SAGE) Project, Inc., in San Francisco was founded in 1992 by the late Norma Hotaling. A self-described survivor of commercial sexual exploitation and heroin addiction, Hotaling sought to end the commercial sex industry and founded SAGE so that other women could live their lives free of sexual exploitation, addiction, and trauma. SAGE staff and case managers self-identified as the experts in exploitation and felt that they were the only organization in the San Francisco Bay Area willing to talk about young people's involvement in trafficking. They felt strongly about referring to this involvement as "trafficking," not "prostitution" or "sex work," and strove to be consistent in this message so that the community and other service providers would also learn to see involvement in the sex industry as human trafficking. Many of the young people SAGE worked with were mandated to the program and were involved in the juvenile justice or child welfare systems.

The funding from OVC allowed SAGE to expand its services to a wider array of young people. Prior to this relationship, SAGE's work with youth was restricted by other funding sources to serving only cisgender girls from San Francisco County. With the OVC funding, cisgender young men, transgender youth, and those living outside of San Francisco County were also made eligible for services at SAGE. Although the OVC funding allowed SAGE to work with cisgender boys and transgender youth, all but one of the clients the agency served while I was doing my research for this project were cisgender girls.

Individual case management was available to all young people at SAGE. During the project period, the number of case managers at SAGE who worked with youth ranged from one to three. As part of its funding, SAGE also provided outreach and training to law enforcement, service providers, and the community about sex trafficking of domestic minors.

SAGE operated two youth programs for girls who were involved in sex trafficking or who were considered to be at risk for involvement. The Life Skills Program worked with youth to help them meet their fundamental needs, build their self-esteem, and guide them toward building healthier relationships with peers and adults. This program met weekly, and its curriculum focused on sexual exploitation, domestic violence, trauma, sexual abuse, and job skills. The group was envisioned as a space where cisgender girls could talk about what was going on in the community and receive help from the program's counselors. Most clients were involved in the Life Skills Program for six to twelve months. Once a client graduated from the Life Skills Program, it was her decision whether to continue to receive services from SAGE and enroll in its adult program. Case managers reported that most young women did not stay connected once they graduated. SAGE's In-Custody Peer Counseling also provided a life skills program as well as individual and group counseling to cisgender girls who were in custody in the juvenile justice system. Youth were not required to go to the group. The group size ranged from two to eighteen. Topics of focus included health, teen dating, and prostitution.

As of September 2014, SAGE closed and is no longer offering services.

ILLINOIS: THE STOP-IT PROGRAM AT THE SALVATION ARMY

The Salvation Army STOP-IT Program in Chicago was founded in 2006. STOP-IT was initially focused on foreign victims of trafficking but expanded its scope to provide outreach and services to domestic youth of all genders who have been or are currently involved in sex trafficking. Although the program does not have a physical space that young people can access, the staff are able to provide case management to their clients by meeting them in locations such as their homes, schools, or fast-food restaurants. STOP-IT also offers a twenty-four/seven response to client emergencies and emergency calls from law enforcement. The majority of clients are referred through law enforcement agencies and hospital emergency rooms. Even though STOP-IT has built a strong relationship with the Chicago Police Department, it does not work with mandated clients.

The Salvation Army started in 1865, and in its earliest work organized homes for "fallen women" who were involved in prostitution or at risk for becoming involved. Its guiding philosophy can be seen in much of STOP-IT's work with youth.

Although STOP-IT does not assume that its clients are ready to exit the sex industry, staff are explicit with their clients that this is their hoped-for outcome. Case managers start their work with what looks like a mentoring relationship. They meet their clients and work with them on their most pressing needs, such as housing, food, and clothing. Once the person's basic needs are addressed, case managers strive to work with them on the next steps that will create ways for them to survive that do not include trading sex. Because STOP-IT is a Salvation Army program, it will not financially assist in providing certain services the young person may request, such as an abortion. However, if youth are looking for such a resource, the case managers will refer them to agencies that provide a wide array of services, and the young persons can go there to learn more about their options. Over the project period, the number of case managers at STOP-IT ranged from three to five.

In addition to case management, STOP-IT also runs an in-custody program and conducts outreach and training to raise awareness about the sexual exploitation of minors. The in-custody program comprises eight weeks of a curriculum that focuses on topics such as sex trafficking and prostitution, Internet safety, and healthy relationships. STOP-IT works to raise awareness about trafficking through training targeted at social service providers, law enforcement personnel, and medical providers. In training and events, STOP-IT representatives go over the definitions of trafficking and then focuses specifically on domestic issues and the involvement of domestic minors. They speak about how youth become involved, warning signs to look for, and the goals of their program.

NEW YORK: THE STREETWORK PROJECT AT SAFE HORIZON

Safe Horizon in New York was established in 1978 to prevent violence and promote justice for victims of crimes and abuse. In 1984, Safe Horizon founded the Streetwork Project to provide services to homeless and street-involved young people of all genders up to twenty-four years of age. Young people involved in sex trades and served by OVC funding are a part of the Streetwork Project rather than in a separate program. Streetwork provides an array of services at two drop-in centers, one in Harlem and the other on the Lower East Side, as well as one residential program that offers short-term, emergency housing for up to twenty-four young people. In the drop-in centers and residential programs, services are provided both by Streetwork staff (e.g., case management, counseling, meals) and by outside agencies that provide on-site services (e.g., medical, psychiatric, legal). Streetwork maintains a strong commitment to a low-threshold, harm reduction philosophy, which translates to a nonjudgmental, client-centered approach. Young people are not judged on their behavior, nor are they pressured to work on any particular area. They are assumed to be competent to make the best choices for their lives, with self-determination as a guiding principle. Streetwork does not work with mandated clients.

Both drop-in centers serve as a space where youth can hang out and access services. Clients choose which drop-in center they will use and are subsequently assigned a case manager who will work with them to assess their needs and facilitate access to services. Over the research project period, the number of case managers at Streetwork who worked directly with this group of young people ranged from four to nine. Most services are provided onsite and include individual and group counseling, advocacy, emergency and crisis housing, GED preparation and support, help in obtaining identification, and help in obtaining Medicaid and other benefits. Legal, medical, and psychiatric services are also provided by outside agencies onsite. At the drop-in centers, young people also have access to hot meals, showers, laundry equipment, and clothing. The drop-in center located on the Lower East Side of Manhattan differs from its Uptown counterpart in some ways. It is much smaller and offers reduced hours of service. One important difference between the two centers is the young people being served at each. Youth at the Lower East Side center have higher rates of drug use and injection drug use. Services provided only at this center include syringe exchange and overdose prevention training.

In addition to the drop-in centers, Streetwork also operates an outreach program at night from 9:00 p.m. to 5:00 a.m. Teams of staff go to different locations throughout the city where homeless youth are known to hang out. The outreach staff let young people know about Streetwork and provide the youth with safe-sex supplies, food, and clothing. The majority of young people who access services at Streetwork are referred either by their peers or through street outreach.

APPENDIX B

METHODOLOGICAL PROCESS

The interviews with program staff at SAGE, STOP-IT, and Streetwork were collected as part of a process evaluation conducted by a team of researchers at RTI International (Deborah Gibbs, Shari Miller, Jennifer Hardison Walters, Marianne Kluckman, and me). The goals of the larger process evaluation were to document components of program implementation in the three programs serving domestic minor victims of human trafficking and to identify promising practices for service delivery for this population. For the purposes of this book, I used data from the three sites to help answer the following questions:

- What are the characteristics of young people who trade sex?
- What services do the young people request, and what do they receive?
- What are the challenges case managers experience in their work with this population?

The exploratory nature of my questions lent itself well to a mixed-methods approach. I used quantitative methods to analyze the programs' monthly client data. These data provided information about those young people who received services through the programs. During our semiannual visits with each site, program staff provided us with case history narratives about the young people being served by their programs.

QUANTITATIVE DATA SOURCES

Program staff provided the RTI International evaluation team with deidentified client information. All forms were developed in collaboration with the program sites. Data forms included "Intake Status"; "Client Service Needs and Service Provisions"; and "Closing Status."

The "Intake Status" form included demographic information, social service system involvement, sex trades characteristics, living situation, health information, trauma history, and service needs. This form was completed for every new or reentering client (previously served but case closed) within forty-five days after intake. The data were collected at intake or during the first thirty days after intake or both. If significant new information regarding the client status at intake was disclosed after the first thirty days, a second form was completed with revised information only.

The "Client Service Needs and Service Provision" form described the services needed and provided to the young person. It was completed monthly for each active client by the fifteenth of the following month and depicted activity during the prior calendar month. If no activity with the client occurred during the month, only the first page of the form was completed.

The "Closing Status" form addressed individuals who had explicitly left the program or whose cases were considered closed due to lack of contact. Both the date on which the case was closed and the reason for closing the case were recorded. This form was filled out for all clients whose case had been classified as closed during the reporting month and was completed by the fifteenth of the following month.

Each program sent copies of all forms to the RTI International evaluation team by scanning and emailing them. Forms included program-created client ID numbers but no identifying information. We entered the data, conducted quality-control checks, and consulted with program staff to resolve any questions. In collaboration with the programs, we conducted periodic reviews of data submitted by programs against staff knowledge of cases. Copies of program data were made available to each program in the format they requested.

For the purposes of this book, I used data from the monthly forms that the sites provided from January 1, 2011, through October 31, 2012. The modest numbers of young people served ($n = 78$) and the straightforward nature of the data allowed me to use simple descriptive methods for the quantitative data.

QUALITATIVE DATA SOURCES

We collected case history narratives about the young people being served by the three community-based organizations from case managers and program staff who worked there. The case narratives were gathered during semiannual site visits to each of the three programs between March 2011 and

December 2012. Over the project period, four site visits took place. During each of the first three visits, five case history narratives were collected from each program, for a total of fifteen unique case history narratives per site (n = 45). After the first site visit, updates were collected at subsequent site visits about individuals for whom a case history narrative already existed and who had contact with the program since the previous site visit. Over the project period, a total of sixty-three updates were collected for forty-two clients (thirteen from SAGE, fourteen from STOP-IT, and fifteen from Streetwork). I used all of the data from the case narratives for this book.

Case managers and other staff at the programs selected five young people per each site visit to profile in case history narratives. Recognizing the limited literature about cisgender boys and transgender youth involved in trading sex, and knowing that these programs did not anticipate seeing a substantial number of cisgender boys or transgender youth, program staff provided narratives about all cisgender young men and transgender program participants. To gather information about promising practices, we asked staff to select a successful case, a case that posed challenges, and a case where the young person turned eighteen and aged out of services. A semistructured interview guide was used for the case history narrative interviews (see appendix C). Case history interviews did not include identifying information or any information that could reasonably be linked to a specific person. Program staff used pseudonyms when describing youth. The interviews were audio recorded and transcribed verbatim.

As a conceptual framework my analysis utilized life course theory (LCT), which examines people's lives within structural, social, and cultural contexts (Elder 1998). LCT asserts that people's behaviors and outcomes are the result of a dynamic process that involves the person, environment, and time (Bronfenbrenner 1979; Elder 1994), with choices contingent upon the opportunities and constraints of the social structure and culture (Elder 1998). Glen Elder (1994) offers four central themes that constitute this theory: (1) the link between human lives and their historical times; (2) timing; (3) linked lives; and (4) human agency. All are critical factors that influence the pathways of human life. Although people's decisions are informed by the opportunities and constraints of history and social circumstance, they still construct their own paths throughout their lives based on the decisions and actions they take (Elder 1998). "Life course theory and research alert us to this real world, a world in which lives are lived and where people work out paths of development as best they can" (Elder 1998, 9).

Few studies have been published that directly use LCT to examine young people who trade sex, but studies have used it to examine overlapping populations, such as runaway adolescents (Yoder, Hoyt, and Whitbeck 1998). A benefit of using LCT is that it does not rely on a one-size-fits-all approach to address issues (Godette, Headen, and Ford 2006). Rather, it offers a framework that is broad enough to represent the heterogeneity of experiences of young people who trade sex. LCT allowed my own analysis to account for those times when youth are truly forced against their will to trade sex as well as the structural, social, and cultural contexts that precede young people's decisions to become involved in sex trades.

Key constructs in LCT include time and timing, trajectories and transitions, critical periods, accumulated risks, and cumulative disadvantage (Godette, Headen, and Ford 2006; Lynch and Smith 2005). Dionne Godette and her colleagues (2006) provide an explanation of these constructs. Time allows outcomes and the factors that influence them to be dynamic, and timing is the lifespan of the experience to be understood. What this means for young people who trade sex is that the structural factors that are antecedents to their involvement in commercial sex need to be examined and that the larger lifespan also needs to be explored when attempting to understand their experiences. Initiation into commercial sex cannot be understood in isolation. Trajectories explain the development of an outcome over time, and transitions represent those periods of time that are characterized by change (for example, leaving home). Critical periods involve those stages in an individual's life where exposures to various factors are more likely to have a deleterious impact than if they occurred at another point in time. Initiation to sex trades at certain ages may be more harmful than at others, and particular risk for initiation or reentry into commercial sex may occur after specific life experiences such as being incarcerated or running away. Accumulated risk and cumulative disadvantage encompass exposure to long-term adversity that furthers the likelihood that the person will experience difficulties. Involvement in sex trades may be just one risk factor. Young people's experiences with juvenile justice, familial abuse, limited employment opportunities, and problems in school may put them at future risk for negative life outcomes.

In addition to LCT, my qualitative analysis was also guided by grounded theory (Glaser and Strauss 1967; Strauss and Corbin 1988). The first step of the grounded theory approach was to ask sensitizing questions such as: What is going on here? Who are the actors involved? How do they define the situation? What is the meaning of the situation to them? What are the various actors doing? These questions assisted in understanding the data. Second, conceptual questions were asked: What is the relationship of one concept to another? How do events or actions change over time? What are the larger structural issues here, and how do these issues play into or effect what I am seeing? Such questions helped to make connections between and among concepts. As I read the interview transcripts and summary statements, posed questions, and read more transcripts and updates, I developed the coding categories (Strauss and Corbin 1988).

My initial code list was informed by the five constructs of LCT (time, timing, trajectories, transitions, critical periods, and accumulated risks) as well as by the interview questions. I then derived codes directly from the interview data, and they represented subject areas that, by virtue of the time the respondent spent discussing them or their recurrent nature or both, seemed important. I revised codes as I analyzed more data. I also modified, collapsed, expanded, or dropped codes as I added new codes to the list. (See appendix D for the final code list.) I coded and entered all case narrative transcripts into the qualitative analysis program NVIVO version 9 (developed by QSR International).

I also wrote theoretical and methodological memos, hallmarks of grounded theory methods, throughout the qualitative analysis process (Glaser and Strauss 1967). These memos pertained to factors that influenced young people's involvement in sex trades, critical periods and traumatic events that precipitated transitions in sex trades involvement, youth's service needs, and the ways in which youth interacted with case managers and other service providers. The memos varied in length, often contained direct quotes from the interviews, and were filed according to the code to which they corresponded.

I wrote summary statements for each case history narrative ($n = 45$) and update ($n = 63$) and coded all of the interviews. A colleague checked 20 percent of the transcripts ($n = 22$) to explore the reliability of the coding. We resolved discrepancies or inconsistencies through consensus discussions. The same colleague reviewed the final analysis and did not raise any issues about it.

Certain limitations are inherent to my methods. The youth served by these three programs are neither a random nor a representative sample of young people who trade sex. These youth either self-selected or were mandated to participate in the programs. Gathering case history narratives from the case managers and program staff rather than interviewing the youth directly about their experiences trading sex is another limitation. Because the program sites indicated that the staff did not feel comfortable having their clients interviewed about their experiences trading sex, the staff's more frequent interactions with their clients offered a narrative that would otherwise not be accessible to outsiders. Even with these limitations, because of the hidden nature of this population, the methods used to acquire these data allowed for the building of a knowledge base on the characteristics of young people who trade sex, their service needs, and the challenges of working with them.

To expand the scope of the book and increase its relevance, I incorporated additional data and information that I did not collect from the three programs. Interestingly, many anti-trafficking activists will state that no one is talking about this issue of young people who trade sex. My experience suggests otherwise—seemingly everyone is talking about it. I found that people I wanted to interview about it had been interviewed previously for local TV shows, news articles, and web forums or had written their own thoughts about this issue on various websites. Dating back to the 1980s, a plethora of research has been published about this group of young people. The issue of young people who trade sex likewise routinely comes up at conferences. Some conferences even focus specifically on this issue. Accessing preexisting published resources and attending webinars and conferences provided me with a wealth of information to use. I also conducted several interviews with scholar-activist Minh Dang. I used the same qualitative analysis process with these sources that I used with the case history narratives.

APPENDIX C

CASE NARRATIVE INTERVIEW GUIDE

INTRODUCTION

Review key points from study information sheet (case managers and program staff will receive info sheet via email prior to interview):
This interview is to find out more about youth who have received services who are domestic minor victims of sex trafficking. It is really important that I do not learn the identity of this young person. What is a fake name that you will use throughout this interview? [NAME].

I'll be taking notes, but if you don't mind, I'd also like to record the conversation as a backup for our own use. Is that okay?

Do you have any questions before we begin?
Start recorder.

DEMOGRAPHICS

1. First I'll be asking some basic demographic information about [NAME].
   Age (both initially and if any updated age—a different age than initially indicated [said was older or younger than actual age])
   Gender
   Ethnicity
   U.S. citizen/lawful permanent resident (LPR)
   Guardianship/dependency status
   Living situation
   Teen pregnancy/parenting

INITIAL PRESENTATION, CHARACTERISTICS, AND SERVICES

2. Next are some questions about [NAME]. Initial presentation when you first met him/her.

When and how did [NAME] come into contact with [PROGRAM]?

What was [NAME's] motivation for making contact with [PROGRAM]?

Describe what you initially learned about [NAME] and his/her circumstances.

What was [NAME's] initial demeanor, emotionally and interpersonally? How did s/he come across?

What did you learn initially about what other service sectors [NAME] was involved with? (specific probes for child welfare, juvenile justice, law enforcement, mental health, health/medical)

What did you learn initially about [NAME's] family history?

Maltreatment history

Parent/caregiver substance abuse, mental health problems, criminal behavior, sex trade involvement, teen parent

3. What did you initially learn about [NAME's] sex trade experiences?

Types of sex trades

Age at first experience

Location where trades occurs (city/county)

Resources traded for sex

Relationship to third party (if there is a third party)

Type of force, fraud, or coercion

4. What referrals did you initially make for [NAME]?

To the best of your knowledge, did [NAME] go to the referral source? If yes, perceptions of service quality. If no, barriers to receiving services.

PRESENTATION, CHARACTERISTICS, SERVICES AFTER GETTING TO KNOW YOUTH

5. As you began to better know [NAME],

Did his/her demeanor emotionally/interpersonally change? If so, describe in what ways it changed.

What did you additionally learn about previous service-sector involvement?
What, if anything, did you learn about [NAME's] family history?
What, if anything, did you learn about [NAME's] sex trade experiences?
After your initial work, what additional referrals did you make for [NAME]?

To the best of your knowledge, did [NAME] go to the referred source? If yes, perceptions of service quality? If no, barriers to receiving services?

6. What aspects of [NAME's] case presented as barriers to engaging in services?
For each of these barriers, what might you have done differently, now looking back?

7. What aspects of your program's interactions with [NAME] would you describe as successful?

8. Do you consider [NAME] to be an ongoing or closed case?
(If ongoing) What are your goals for ongoing work with [NAME]?
When was the most recent time that you had contact with [NAME]?
To the best of your knowledge, why is [NAME] no longer in contact with the program?

APPENDIX D

QUALITATIVE ANALYSIS CODE LIST

AGENCY: When young people are described as having agency, choosing certain behaviors/actions. Includes discussions about the person's resiliency and/or resourcefulness.

DEMEANOR: Descriptions about a young person's emotional, interpersonal, and physical presentation. Includes changes in demeanor over time.

DEMOGRAPHICS: Descriptions of young person's gender, race, age, education status, citizenship, sexual identity, and kids.

DRUGS: Drug use or involvement in drug sales. Includes alcohol.

EMPLOYMENT: Descriptions of young person's legal sector job(s).

FAMILY: Biological parents or guardians. Maltreatment by family. Family issues (substance use, mental health issues, poverty). Includes familial history of sex trades.

FORCED LABOR: Nonsexual labor.

FRIENDS: Descriptions of young person's friends.

GRANTEE: Descriptions of the OVC-funded program and its philosophy.

AGE OUT: Narratives about when a young person turns eighteen and not eligible for OVC-funded services.

CASE MANAGEMENT: Descriptions of case management.

CASE MANAGER NEEDS: Services the case managers think the young person needs.

CLIENT NEEDS: Services the young person identifies as wanting.

OUTCOMES: What case managers consider to be successful or troubling outcomes.

REFERRALS: Services the young person is referred to. Includes both internal and external services.

CHALLENGES: Difficulties in working with this population.

MACRO: Describes the culture in which individuals live. For example, policies, homo- and transphobia, sex trade stigma.

MESO: Refers to relations between microsystems or connections between contexts.

MICRO: Refers to the institutions and groups that most immediately and directly impact the young person, including OVC-funded program, family, school, religious institutions, neighborhood, and peers.

PROGRAM SPECIFIC: Problems unique to the structure or functioning of the program.

ENGAGEMENT: Ways in which the young person interacts with overall program. Includes other services the person receives beyond case management. Includes when the young person is no longer accessing services.

ENTRY: How young person first came in contact with the grantee.

HEALTH: Pregnancy, physical health issues (includes disabilities), sexual health issues (sexually transmitted infections/HIV), mental health issues.

INTIMATE RELATIONSHIPS: Description of intimate relationships with others. Can include relationship with a third party.

LIVING SITUATION: Places where the young person lives.

RUNAWAY: Descriptions about running away from home or a system (i.e., juvenile justice placement or foster home).

SELF-ESTEEM: Descriptions about the young person's confidence in self. Includes discussions of shame/stigma.

SEX TRADE INVOLVEMENT:

CLIENTS: Descriptions about the people purchasing sexual services.

THIRD PARTIES: Anyone who connects young people to clients or benefits financially from their involvement. Includes but is not limited to pimps, traffickers, friends, acquaintances, and family.

INITIATION: Details about first experience trading sex. Includes life events associated with involvement in sex trades (LCT: timing).

TRANSITIONS: Experiences moving in and out of sex trade involvement after initiation (LCT: Changes in involvement over time).

STAR: Star quotes. Quotes that illustrate key themes and findings in the analysis and that will likely be used for publications and presentations

SYSTEM INVOLVEMENT: Other services the young person is connected to (by choice or through mandate). Involvement in community.

CBOs: Community-based organizations.
CHILD WELFARE
EDUCATION
HEALTH
HOUSING
JUVENILE JUSTICE
POLICE
RELIGIOUS INSTITUTIONS
VIOLENCE: Young person's experiences with violence. Not limited to violence experienced in connection with sex trades.

APPENDIX E

SAMPLE CHARACTERISTICS

Over the twenty-two months I interacted with staff at SAGE, STOP-IT, and Streetwork, seventy-eight young people were enrolled across the three programs (table apE.1). Each of the programs served clients up to the age of eighteen (range thirteen to eighteen). The median age of all clients was sixteen. Nearly 86 percent of all clients identified as cisgender women (range 60–96 percent). Although the programs were required to serve youth of all genders, only Streetwork served a sizeable proportion of cisgender men (35 percent), and all of the programs struggled to reach transgender youth. Seventy-one percent of all clients identified as African American. Nearly one-quarter of the clients served were legal wards of the court or child welfare. The percentage of young people reported as being in school overstates the actual role of education in their lives. Instead of attendance, this number more accurately reflects enrollment. At the time of intake into the program, only one youth reported being employed. Forty percent were involved in the child welfare system. Across the three programs, the median number of interactions with clients was 10.5 (range 1–221), and the median length of service delivery was 113 days (approximately three and three-quarters months).

See table apE.1.

REFERRAL SOURCES

Each of the three programs had multiple strategies for accessing young people involved in sex trades (figure apE.1). The two main referral sources for SAGE were juvenile justice and probation (24 percent) and child protective services (17 percent). For STOP-IT, the majority of referrals came from law

TABLE AP E.1 SAMPLE CHARACTERISTICS

	SAGE		STOP-IT		STREETWORK		TOTAL	
	n	VALUE	*n*	VALUE	*n*	VALUE	*n*	VALUE
Number of clients	29		29		20		78	
Number of client interactions								
Range		4–85		1-182		1–221		1–221
Median		10		21		4.5		10.5
Length of service (in days)								
Range		4–502		7–405		10–531		4–531
Median		85		119		122		113
Age								
Range		13–18		13–17		13–17		13–18
Median		17		16		16		16
Gender								
Cisgender young men	0	0%	1	3.4%	7	35.0%	8	10.3%
Cisgender young women	28	96.6%	27	93.1%	12	60.0%	67	85.9%
Transgender young men	0	0%	0	0%	0	0%	0	0.0%
Transgender young women	1	3.4%	1	3.4%	1	5.0%	3	3.8%
Race/Ethnicity*								
American Indian or Alaska Native	4	13.8%	0	0%	1	5.0%	5	6.4%
Asian	1	3.4%	0	0%	1	5.0%	2	2.6%
African American	18	62.1%	25	86.2%	12	60.0%	55	70.5%

(continued on next page)

TABLE AP E.1 SAMPLE CHARACTERISTICS

	SAGE		STOP-IT		STREETWORK		TOTAL	
	n	VALUE	*n*	VALUE	*n*	VALUE	*n*	VALUE
Race/Ethnicity* *(continued from previous page)*								
Native Hawaiian or other Pacific Islander	1	3.4%	0	0%	0	0%	1	1.3%
White	6	20.7%	2	6.9%	8	40.0%	16	20.5%
Hispanic/Latino(a)	3	10.3%	5	17.2%	9	45.0%	17	21.8%
Other	5	17.2%	0	0%	0	0%	5	6.4%
Citizenship status								
Citizen	29	100%	28	96.6%	20	100%	77	98.7%
Lawful permanent resident	0	0%	1	3.4%	0	0%	1	1.3%
Legal ward	9	31.0%	6	20.7%	4	20.0%	19	24.4%
Don't know	2	6.9%	0	0%	3	15.0%	5	0.4%
Education and employment								
School only	22	75.9%	15	51.7%	9	45.0%	46	59.0%
Employed only	0	0%	0	0.0%	0	0%	0	0%
Both school and employed	0	0%	1	3.4%	0	0%	1	1.3%
Neither	7	24.1%	13	44.8%	11	55.0%	31	39.7%
Current systems involvement								
Child welfare	14	48.3%	10	34.5%	7	35.0%	31	39.7%
Juvenile justice	18	62.1%	7	24.1%	3	15.0%	28	35.9%

* MULTIPLE CHOICES WERE ALLOWED.

FIGURE AP E.1 THREE PROGRAMS' INFORMAL AND FORMAL CLIENT REFERRAL SOURCES.

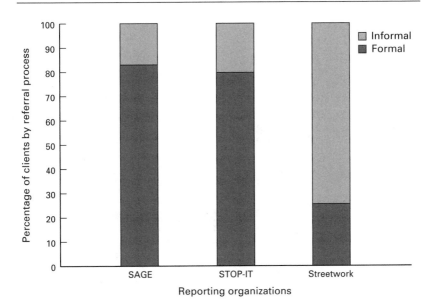

enforcement officials (38 percent) and hospital staff (17 percent). Referrals into Streetwork were primarily through informal sources such as word of mouth and peer referral (45 percent) and self-referral following street outreach encounters (20 percent).

As part of the referral sources, 17 percent of SAGE's clients were court mandated to the program. Although STOP-IT reported not working with mandated clients, one of their clients was mandated to the program; no clients were mandated to Streetwork.

LIVING SITUATION

At the time of their intake into the program, young people reported all the places they had lived in the previous thirty days. Few youth reported living in child welfare group homes or foster homes (figure apE.2). Many young people, especially those being served by STOP-IT and SAGE, were either living in family or system settings. In contrast, the majority of Streetwork clients were marginally housed or were homeless. Overall, the data for the three programs largely understate the transient nature of living situations.

FIGURE AP E.2 LIVING SITUATION(S) REPORTED BY CLIENTS AT TIME OF INTAKE IN THE THREE PROGRAMS.

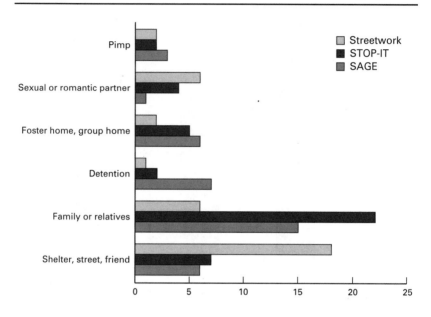

Half of all clients reported multiple types of living situations, and others may have experienced multiple settings of the same type—bouncing among family members, for example.

SEX TRADE CHARACTERISTICS

Based on the intake data, the median age at which young people first traded sex was fifteen (table apE.2). Although 40 percent of all clients were still engaged in sex trades at the time of their intake, current involvement trading sex was primarily among Streetwork clients. Data not shown in table apE.2 reveal that more than half (53 percent) reported connecting with clients on the street (range 25–76 percent), 39 percent through the Internet (range 20–59 percent), and 28 percent through informal mechanisms such as a peer connection or an unplanned encounter (range 24–30 percent).

The majority of Streetwork clients did not have a third party connected to their involvement in trading sex, which is markedly different from

TABLE AP E.2 SEX TRADE CHARACTERISTICS

	SAGE		STOP-IT		STREETWORK		TOTAL	
	n	VALUE	*n*	VALUE	*n*	VALUE	*n*	VALUE
Total clients	29		29		20		78	
Currently trading sex	7	24.1%	7	24.1%	17	85.0%	31	39.7%
Age at first sex trade								
Range		10–17		10–17		10–17		10–17
Median		14		15		15.5		15
Sex trade facilitator relationship*								
None; client arranged for self	9	31.0%	2	6.9%	16	80.0%	27	34.6%
Sexual or romantic partner	5	17.2%	3	10.3%	0	0%	8	10.3%
Friend or acquaintance or peer	5	17.2%	6	20.7%	2	10.0%	13	16.7%
Family household member	1	3.4%	3	10.3%	0	0%	4	5.1%
Gang	0	0%	2	6.9%	0	0%	2	2.6%
Pimp	16	55.2%	14	48.3%	3	15.0%	33	42.3%
Someone else	0	0%	1	3.4%	0	0%	1	1.3%
Don't know	5	17.2%	4	13.8%	6	30.0%	15	19.2%

* MULTIPLE CHOICES WERE ALLOWED.

the experiences of youth connected with STOP-IT and SAGE. A variety of people acted as third parties. Across the three programs, 42 percent of clients reported having a pimp. Qualitative interviews with program staff revealed the infrequency with which young people considered people in their lives as pimps. Therefore, the quantitative finding about pimps may reflect the case managers' rather than their clients' perspective about the nature of the relationships. As one case manager said, "Everything about it

FIGURE AP E.3 RESOURCES EXCHANGED FOR SEX REPORTED BY CLIENTS IN THE THREE PROGRAMS.

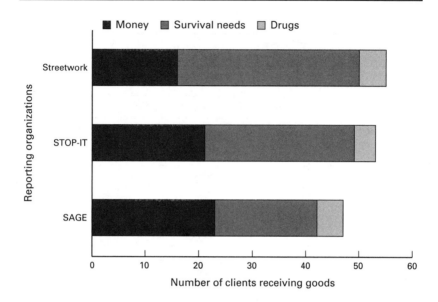

is pimp except what she calls him" (E. Dalberg, personal communication, November 1, 2011).

RESOURCES EXCHANGED FOR SEX

Clients could report more than one response to what they received in exchange for sex (figure apE.3). The overwhelming majority cited money (77 percent). In combination, items that are best classified as survival needs (food, clothing, shelter, protection) were the next most-cited resources. A small portion of youth also received drugs in exchange for sex.

TYPES OF FORCE, FRAUD, OR COERCION IN SEX TRADE INVOLVEMENT

In various ways, this group of young people experienced force, fraud, or coercion in connection with their sex trades (figure apE.4). Overall, 44 percent

FIGURE AP E.4 TYPES OF FORCE, FRAUD, OR COERCION EXPERIENCED IN CONNECTION WITH SEX TRADES REPORTED BY CLIENTS IN THE THREE PROGRAMS.

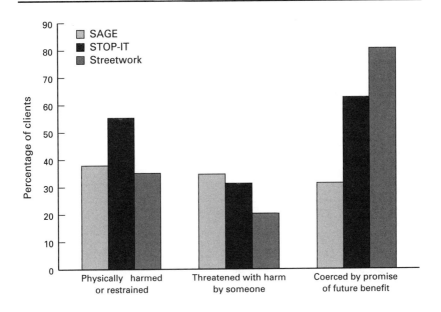

reported ever being physically harmed or restrained, 30 percent were threatened with harm, and 55 percent were coerced by promise of future benefit.

CHARACTERISTICS OF YOUNG PEOPLE PROFILED IN CASE NARRATIVES

Over the project period, fifteen unique case history narratives were collected from each program, for a total of forty-five individual case narratives. A total of sixty-three updates were collected for forty-two clients. The median age at intake for the case narrative sample was sixteen (table apE.3). Because program staff were asked to include all cisgender men and transgender youth for the case history narratives, their percentages are noticeably higher than those of the overall sample. For the clients included in the qualitative data, across the three programs the median number of interactions with clients was twenty-four (range 1–181), and the median length of service delivery was 189 days (approximately six and one-third months). The case history narratives were collected from case managers and program staff who worked with the youth.

TABLE AP E.3 CASE NARRATIVE SAMPLE CHARACTERISTICS

	SAGE		STOP-IT		STREETWORK		TOTAL	
	n	VALUE	*n*	VALUE	*n*	VALUE	*n*	VALUE
Total clients	15		15		15		45	
Total number of client interactions								
Range	3–156		1–181		3–90		1–181	
Median	28		32		10		24	
Length of service (in days)								
Range	4–502		51–405		10–531		4–531	
Median	216		177		182		189	
Age								
Range	13–18		13–17		13–17		13–18	
Median	17		16		17		16	
Gender								
Cisgender young men	0	0%	2	13.3%	7	46.7%	9	20.0%
Cisgender young women	15	100.0%	12	80.0%	7	46.7%	34	75.6%
Transgender young men	0	0%	0	0%	0	0%	0	0%
Transgender young women	0	0%	1	6.7%	1	6.7%	2	4.4%
Race/Ethnicity*								
American Indian or Alaska Native	1	6.7%	0	0%	0	0%	1	2.2%
Asian	0	0%	0	10–17	0	10–17	0	10–17
African American	7	46.7%	14	93.3%	4	26.7%	25	55.6%
Native Hawaiian or other Pacific Islander	0	0%	0	0%	1	6.7%	1	2.2%
White	5	33.3%	1	6.7%	7	46.7%	13	28.9%
Hispanic/Latino(a)/Spanish	2	13.3%	1	6.7%	9	60.0%	12	26.7%
Friend or acquaintance or peer	5	17.2%	6	20.7%	2	10.0%	13	16.7%
Other	5	33.3%	0	0%	2	13.3%	7	15.6%
Citizenship status								
Citizen	15	100.0%	15	100.0%	15	100.0%	45	100.0%
Lawful permanent resident	0	0%	0	0%	0	0%	0	0%

* MULTIPLE CHOICES WERE ALLOWED.

NOTES

1. INTRODUCTION

1. The TVPA offers two versions of trafficking: "severe forms of trafficking in persons" and "sex trafficking." Section 103.9 articulates that the designation *sex trafficking* means "the recruitment, harboring, transportation, provision, or obtaining of a person for the purpose of a commercial sex act." This separate definition for sex trafficking is representative of the "ideological opposition to sex work" in the United States (Zimmerman 2013, 161).
2. Please see chapter 3 for a detailed discussion about my choice to use the term *third-party involvement* as opposed to *pimp* or *trafficker*.
3. This definition is largely shared by the United Nations Protocol to Prevent, Suppress and Punish Trafficking in Persons, Especially Women and Children, of which the United States is a signatory. More commonly referred to as the United Nations Trafficking in Persons Protocol, it was adopted in 2000 and entered into force in 2003.
4. Although the definition for *severe forms of trafficking in persons* was put forth in the TVPA, it was not until the TVPRA of 2005 that more attention was paid to domestic minors. This reauthorization allocated funding to agencies that worked with young people in the United States who had experienced trafficking. It also established a pilot program charged with providing residential facilities, services, and benefits for these young people.
5. The William Wilberforce Trafficking Victims Protection Reauthorization Act of 2008 recognized that some young people who experienced trafficking were being held in restrictive placements and indicated that youth should be given the least-restrictive placements possible unless they are a danger to the community or are charged with a crime.
6. The 2013 reauthorization was included as an amendment to the Violence Against Women Reauthorization Act of 2013, Pub. L. No. 113-4.
7. This focus on cisgender women and girls continues today, with cisgender boys and transgender youth noticeably absent from academic articles, conference presentations, and media stories. Although some researchers and commentators now add

the phrase "and boys too" to their discussions about young people who trade sex (Friedman 2013), most discussions "nearly always specify 'she,' 'her,' or 'the girl' as if no boy" has ever been involved in the sex trade (Dennis 2008, 12).

8. In 1911, the Immigration Commission found the Mann Act problematic because it excluded men and boys as potential victims. In 1977, this problem was resolved when the Protection of Children Against Sexual Exploitation Act amended the Mann Act to apply to boys also. The U.S. Immigration Commission, authorized by Congress in 1891, is charged with investigating U.S. immigration laws. From 1907 to 1910, the commission was also known as the Dillingham Commission. Its report in 1911 evaluated the Mann Act.

9. Because the Mann Act requires an element of transportation, it limits its prosecution to cases where movement across state of national lines can be proven. As a consequence, in current cases involving young people who trade sex, if no movement across state or national lines occurred, the Mann Act is not applicable.

10. The 1986 amendment of the Mann Act replaced the phrase "any other immoral purpose" with "any sexual activity for which any person can be charged with a criminal offense" (Pub L. No. 99-628, 100 Stat. 3511–3512).

11. *Caminetti v. United States*, 242 U.S. 470 (1917), https://supreme.justia.com/cases/federal/us/242/470/case.html.

12. *United States v. Holte*, 236 U.S. 140 (1915), https://supreme.justia.com/cases/federal/us/236/140/case.html.

13. *Policy and procedure: White Slave Traffic Act*, No. 66-6200-31, September 15, 1949.

14. For the data tables of the 2013 NIBRS, see http://www.fbi.gov/about-us/cjis/ucr/nibrs/2013/data-tables.

15. Young people who trade sex are considered a hidden population. Because no list of all the young people who trade sex exists, the size of the group is unknown, and researchers may never be able to have a random sample of the entire population. Research about these youth relies on convenience samples that provide characteristics about that sample but are not necessarily generalizable to other groups of young people. As a consequence, data about race and socioeconomic status are limited in that they do not represent the entirety of young people who trade sex in the United States but rather the specific subpopulation that has been sampled.

3. LINKED LIVES

1. It is important to address the racially coded nature of the term *gorilla pimp*. The United States has a history of racial oppression inclusive of dehumanizing blacks by depicting them as apelike. The outcomes of such dehumanization include the "target[ing] [of certain social groups] for cruelty, social degradation, and state-sanctioned violence" (Goff et al. 2008, 305). Although explicit representations that depict blacks as apelike are not nearly as prevalent as they once were, we have re-

cent examples of this dehumanization. The term "no humans involved" (NHI) is an example of a dehumanizing term that police use to describe or reference crimes committed against certain people (Almodovar 2002; Wynter 1992). As recently as the 1990s, "public officials of the judicial system of Los Angeles routinely used the acronym N.H.I. to refer to any case involving a breach of the rights of young Black males" (Wynter 1992, 42). Another example is found in the words of one of the police officers involved in beating Rodney King. Prior to his involvement in the beating, the officer had been responding to a domestic dispute that involved a black couple. Talking about that domestic dispute, the officer commented that it was "right out of *Gorillas in the Mist*" (Associated Press 1991).

Research by Phillip Goff and his colleagues (2008) illustrates the social and political consequences of the racial association between blacks and apes. White male undergraduates were shown a video of a police beating and then were asked to what degree they felt the police violence was justified. Those who saw words associated with apes before viewing the video felt the officers' actions were more justified. In their review of 153 death-eligible cases in Philadelphia, the researchers found that journalists were more likely to use animal language to describe black defendants than they were to describe white defendants. In addition, those black people who were sentenced to death were more likely to be described as apelike in news coverage compared to those who were not sentenced to death. Jennifer Eberhardt, Stanford associate professor of psychology and MacArthur Foundation Fellow, explained the implications of these research findings, "So not only are Blacks associated with apes, but this association is linked to justifications of violence and death" (qtd. in Perlberg 2011).

5. MESOSYSTEM CHALLENGES

1. Perhaps in response to the documented limitations of the child welfare system, Section 101 of the Preventing Sex Trafficking and Strengthening Families Act of 2014 requires all states to have policies and procedures in their child welfare plans for identifying, documenting, and providing appropriate services to young people in state care who are at risk of or have experienced sex trafficking.
2. Specific services, such as housing, are notably absent in all geographic locations (Clawson and Grace 2007; Gragg et al. 2007). The lack of housing is more fully explored in chapter 7.

6. FROM CRIMINALIZATION TO DECRIMINALIZATION

1. It is important to note one of the limitations of the FBI's UCR data. In my analysis of this data, I noticed that the numbers reported for a specific year do not match the numbers reported for that year in the table that looks at trends over a ten-year

period. In 2004, for example, 891 prostitution-related arrests of young people were reported. In the table from 2013 that includes a reference to the arrest rates for 2004, however, the FBI reported 1,157 prostitution-related arrests of youth. This number is 30 percent larger than the number reported in 2004. To date I have not been able to determine why this discrepancy exists.

2. The TVPRA of 2008 mandated the collection of arrest data for human trafficking offenses. In January 2013, the UCR Program began collecting this data. Although one can expect that it will take time for agencies to find the necessary resources for data collection, it is surprising that seemingly minimal effort was devoted to this requirement during the four years between the enactment of the TVPRA of 2008 and the initiation of data collection. For 2013, only five counties in four states added the capability to collect human trafficking data (U.S. FBI 2015). Therefore, the data are not generalizable. To provide some context, California was not one of the states collecting human trafficking data for the UCR in 2013. However, in 2013 California's Department of Justice reported 195 prostitution arrests of minors (females accounted for 183 of those arrests).

3. The monthly returns are given at http://www.fbi.gov/about-us/cjis/ucr/reporting-forms/monthly-return-of-human-trafficking-offenses-known-to-law-enforcement. The email address for queries is crimestatsinfo@ic.fbi.gov.

4. The *Trafficking in Persons Report* for 2012 highlights how even though state and local law enforcement officials have received "numerous trainings on victim identification . . . , [nongovernmental organizations] noted that some federal, state, and local law enforcement officials were reluctant to identify individuals as trafficking victims when they have participated in criminal activity" (U.S. Department of State 2012, 363).

5. The same findings maintain when we look outside the United States. In England, younger youth and those who are coerced by a third party to trade sex are more likely to be considered victims. Those trading sex for survival or in other ways seeming to be complicit in their involvement in sex trades are not deemed worthy of a victim status (Chase and Statham 2004; Phoenix 2002).

6. This gendered approach is also revealed in the placement of the TVPRA of 2013 as an amendment to the Violence Against Women Act. This placement frames human trafficking as a women's rights issue and positions men as perpetrators or perpetrators-to-be (Dang 2013). The gendered approach is also evident in the United Nations Trafficking in Persons Protocol (United Nations 2000), which emphasizes women and children at the expense of men.

7. The text of section 647(b) can be found at http://law.onecle.com/california/penal/647.html.

8. The text of California Assembly Bill 22 can be found at http://www.leginfo.ca.gov/pub/05–06/bill/asm/ab_0001–0050/ab_22_bill_20050921_chaptered.pdf.

9. The text of California Assembly Bill 17 can be found at http://leginfo.legislature.ca.gov/faces/billNavClient.xhtml?bill_id=200920100AB17.

10. The text of California Assembly Bill 12 can be found at http://leginfo.legislature. ca.gov/faces/billNavClient.xhtml?bill_id=201120120AB12.

11. The text of California Assembly Bill 90 can be found at http://leginfo.legislature. ca.gov/faces/billNavClient.xhtml?bill_id=201120120AB90.

12. The text of California Proposition 35 can be found at http://www.kcet.org/news/ ballotbrief/elections2012/propositions/prop-35-read-the-text.html. Proposition 35 was voter initiated. When it was placed on the ballot, California state senators had a history of addressing trafficking and were at work on additional antitrafficking legislation. It is rare to have voter-initiated legislation when the issue is already being addressed by the state. It is worth noting that section 2 of the proposition cites the flawed estimate of three hundred thousand young people at risk of sex trafficking (Estes and Weiner 2005) and gives the average age of entry into trading sex as between twelve and fourteen. Both of these data, the scope of the issue and the average age of entry, were critically examined in the introduction. It is problematic to have state legislation based on flawed data.

13. The text of the Illinois Safe Children Act can be found at http://www.ilga.gov/legis-lation/96/HB/PDF/09600HB6462ham001.pdf.

14. The SHA text can be found at http://www.njjn.org/uploads/digital-library/3175. pdf.

15. The TVPA, its reauthorizations, and the United Nations Trafficking in Persons Protocol all prioritize law enforcement responses over human rights provisions.

16. This suggestion is reflected in the Preventing Sex Trafficking and Strengthening Families Act of 2014, where, as explained previously, all states must have policies and procedures in their child welfare plans for young people who trade sex or are at risk of trading sex. Curiously, section 102 of this act requires that any time a child welfare agency receives information that a youth has experienced sex trafficking, the agency must report to law enforcement within twenty-four hours of receiving that information. The rationale behind this mandated reporting is unclear.

7. MACROSYSTEM CHALLENGES

1. In addition to housing, other approved activities for these grants include providing young people with a twenty-four-hour emergency social service response, clothing and other daily needs, case management services, mental health services, legal services, training for providers, treatment programs that are geared toward people charged or cited with purchasing or attempting to purchase sex, and outreach and education programs that focus on deterring and preventing young people from trading sex.

2. The text of the Runaway and Homeless Youth Act can be found at http://www.gpo .gov/fdsys/pkg/PLAW-110publ378/pdf/PLAW-110publ378.pdf.

3. The Runaway and Homeless Youth Act was most recently reauthorized in 2008. As of October 2014, it is on the legislative calendar for reauthorization. If approved, it will be called the Runaway and Homeless Youth and Trafficking Prevention Act (https://www.congress.gov/bill/113th-congress/senate-bill/2646). The reauthorization would require: (1) shelters to provide services for young people who have experienced trafficking or sexual exploitation; (2) plans to ensure that those who have experienced trafficking or sexual exploitation are provided referrals to comprehensive services; (3) an amendment to the Victims of Child Abuse Act of 1990 by including human trafficking and production of child pornography in the definition of child abuse; (4) an amendment to the TVPA by including patronizing or soliciting a person for a commercial sex act in the definition of sex trafficking; and (5) the enhancement or establishment of court programs for trafficking victims that would require regular appearances and compliance with court-ordered treatment.

8. CONCLUSION

1. This aspect of the model state statute addresses how some state laws require the proof of force, fraud, or coercion when young people are trading sex (Butler 2014).
2. The text of Kentucky Senate Bill 184 is given at http://openstates.org/ky/bills/2014RS/SB184/.
3. My experience that evidence-based research is lacking on international responses to young people who trade sex mirrors that of the Institute of Medicine and the National Research Council (2013). I was able to triangulate different data sources about what is happening in India and therefore am including these data in this text.
4. The text for the United Nations Convention on the Rights of the Child, adopted in 1989 and coming into force in 1990, is given at http://www.ohchr.org/en/professionalinterest/pages/crc.aspx.

REFERENCES

ABC News. 2006. Teen girls' stories of sex trafficking in U.S. February 9. http://abcnews.go.com/Primetime/story?id=1596778&page=1.

Abdullah, H. 2014. Sold into sex slavery: Lawmakers work to end underground sex trafficking. *CNN*, May 21. http://www.cnn.com/2014/05/20/politics/sex-trafficking-bills/.

Adler, L. 2003. An essay on the production of youth prostitution. In symposium on law, labor, and gender, *Maine Law Review* 55 (1): 191–209.

Agustín, L. M. 2007. *Sex at the margins: Migration, labour markets, and the rescue industry*. London: Zed Books.

Almodovar, N. J. 2002. For their own good: The results of the prostitution laws as enforced by cops, politicians, and judges. In W. McElroy, ed., *Liberty for women: Freedom and feminism in the twenty-first century*, 71–87. Oakland, Calif.: Independent Institute.

Amber, J. 2010. Black girls for sale. *Essence*, October, 164–170.

American Bar Association. 2011. ABA policies on human trafficking. http://www.americanbar.org/groups/human_rights/projects/task_force_human_trafficking/policies_on_humantrafficking.html.

Anderson, J. A. 2000. The need for interagency collaboration for children with emotional and behavioral disabilities and their families. *Families in Society* 81 (5): 484–493.

Annitto, M. 2011. Consent, coercion, and compassion: Emerging legal responses to the commercial sexual exploitation of minors. *Yale Law & Policy Review* 30:1–70.

Aradau, C. 2004. The perverse politics of four-letter words: Risk and pity in the securitisation of human trafficking. *Millennium—Journal of International Studies* 33 (2): 251–277.

Associated Press. 1991. Judge says remarks on "gorillas" may be cited in trial on beating. *New York Times*, June 12. http://www.nytimes.com/1991/06/12/us/judge-says-remarks-on-gorillas-may-be-cited-in-trial-on-beating.html.

Bagheri, P. 2013. Anatomy of a child sex trafficking case. Paper presented at the San Francisco Collaborative Against Human Trafficking 2013 Conference to End Child Sex Trafficking, San Francisco, August.

Ball, M. 2005. Authorities clash over handling of teens arrested for prostitution. *Las Vegas Sun*, April 5. http://www.lasvegassun.com/news/2005/apr/05/authorities-clash-over-handling-of-teens-arrested-/.

Banks, D., and T. Kyckelhahn. 2011. *Characteristics of suspected human trafficking incidents*. Washington, D.C.: Bureau of Justice Statistics.

Banovic, B., and Z. Bjelajac. 2012. Traumatic experiences, psychophysical consequences, and needs of human trafficking victims. *Vojnosanitetski Pregled* 69 (1): 94–97.

Barry, K. 1979. *Female sexual slavery*. Englewood Cliffs, N.J.: Prentice-Hall.

Barry, P. J., J. Ensign, and S. H. Lippek. 2002. Embracing street culture: Fitting health care into the lives of street youth. *Journal of Transcultural Nursing* 13 (2): 145–152.

Baskin, S. 2014a. Collateral damage: Sex workers and anti-trafficking campaigns. Paper presented at the Freedom Network Annual Conference, San Francisco, March–April.

——. 2014b. Justice and dignity for survivors through vacating convictions. Paper presented at the Freedom Network Annual Conference, San Francisco, March–April.

Beckman, M. D. 1984. Note: The White Slave Traffic Act: The historical impact of a criminal law policy on women. *Georgetown Law Journal* 72:1111–1139.

Bernstein, N., and L. K. Foster. 2008. *Voices from the street: A survey of homeless youth by their peers*. Sacramento: California Research Bureau.

Best, J. 1997. Victimization and the victim industry. *Society* 34 (4): 9–17.

Birge, E., K. Chon, C. Dukes, and J. Littrel. 2013. The commercial sexual exploitation of children (CSEC): What schools need to know to understand and respond to human trafficking. National Center for Homeless Education Webinar Series, December 4. http://center.serve.org/nche/downloads/webinar/csec.pdf.

Birkhead, T. R. 2011. The "youngest profession": Consent, autonomy, and prostituted children. *Washington University Law Review* 88 (5): 1055–1115.

Black, D. J. 1980. *The manners and customs of the police*. New York: Academic Press.

Bourdieu, P. 1984. *Distinction: A social critique of the judgment of taste*. Cambridge, Mass.: Harvard University Press.

Brawn, K. M., and S. D. Roe. 2008. Female juvenile prostitutes: Exploring the relationship to substance use. *Children and Youth Services Review* 30 (12): 1395–1402.

Brennan, D. 2014. Outside-in: Inspiring change through collaboration. Paper presented at the Freedom Network Annual Conference, San Francisco, March–April.

Brittle, K. 2008. Child abuse by another name: Why the child welfare system is the best mechanism in place to address the problem of juvenile prostitution. *Hofstra Law Review* 36 (4): 1339–1375.

Bronfenbrenner, U. 1979. *The ecology of human development: Experiments by nature and design*. Cambridge, Mass.: Harvard University Press.

Brown, E., G. C. Rodriguez, and A. Smith. 2010. *100 girls: A preliminary look at the lives and outcomes of young women incarcerated in San Francisco Juvenile Hall*. San Francisco: Youth Justice Institute.

Brown, G. O. 2008. Little girl lost: Las Vegas Metro Police Vice Division and the use of material witness holds against teenaged prostitutes. *Catholic University Law Review* 57 (2): 471–509.

Bullard, J., and D. Wygal, prod. 2014. *Human trafficking: Identify and respond*. DVD. Sacramento: California Commission on POST.

Burns, B. J., and R. M. Friedman. 1990. Examining the research base for child mental health services and policy. *Journal of Mental Health Administration* 17:87–98.

Burns, T. 2014. I'm Kathy Pollitt's "highly educated" leftist—and a sex trafficking victim. *Tits and Sass*, May 22. http://titsandsass.com/im-katha-pollitts-highly-educated-leftist-and-a-sex-trafficking-victim/.

Burwick, A., V. Oddo, L. Durso, D. Friend, and G. Gates. 2014. *Identifying and serving LGBTQ youth: Case studies of runaway and homeless youth program grantees*. Washington, D.C.: U.S. Department of Health & Human Services.

Busch-Armendariz, N., M. Nsonwu, and L. C. Heffron. 2009. Understanding human trafficking: Development of typologies of traffickers, phase II. Paper presented at the Interdisciplinary Conference on Human Trafficking, Lincoln, Neb., October.

Butler, C. N. 2014. Making the grade? The United States' TIP report card on child sex trafficking. *SMU Law Review* 67:341–369.

California Homeless Youth Project. 2011. *Programs serving California's homeless youth: Results of a point-in-time survey*. Sacramento: California Homeless Youth Project.

Californians Against Sexual Exploitation. 2012. What is human trafficking? http://www.caseact.org/wp-content/uploads/2012/07/Prop-35-Human-Trafficking-Fact-Sheet.pdf.

Callahan, M., and L. Schroeder. 2014. Sex traffickers often target troubled local teens. *Bucks County Courier Times*, September 28. http://www.buckscountycouriertimes.com/tabs/hidden-victims/sex-traffickers-often-target-troubled-local-teens/article_b8bc090d-1941-57d8-8b06-afa38b956069.html.

Calvin, E. 2010. *My so-called emancipation: From foster care to homelessness for California youth*. New York: Human Rights Watch.

Campano, E. 2013. Are evangelicals monopolizing, misleading US anti-trafficking efforts? *Patheos: Hosting the Conversation on Faith*, January 17. http://www.patheos.com/blogs/religionnow/2013/01/are-evangelicals-monopolizing-misleading-us-anti-trafficking-efforts/#ixzz3Qbo9VekW.

Cates, J. A. 1989. Adolescent male prostitution by choice. *Child & Adolescent Social Work Journal* 6 (2): 151–156.

Chaffee, T. 2013. Anatomy of a child sex trafficking case. Paper presented at the San Francisco Collaborative Against Human Trafficking 2013 Conference to End Child Sex Trafficking, August, San Francisco.

Chang, G., and K. Kim. 2007. Reconceptualizing approaches to human trafficking: New directions and perspectives from the field(s). *Stanford Journal of Civil Rights and Civil Liberties* 3 (2): 317–344. Loyola-LA Legal Studies Paper no. 2007-2047.

Chase, E., and J. Statham. 2004. *The commercial sexual exploitation of children and young people: An overview of key literature and data*. London: Thomas Coram Research Unit, Institute of Education, University of London.

Chettiar, J., K. Shannon, E. Wood, R. Zhang, and T. Kerr. 2010. Survival sex work involvement among street-involved youth who use drugs in a Canadian setting. *American Journal of Public Health* 32 (3): 322–327.

Chicago Alliance Against Sexual Exploitation. 2013. Prevention. http://caase.org/prevention.

Chon, K. 2013. The commercial sexual exploitation of children: What schools need to know to understand and respond to human trafficking. National Center for Homeless Education Webinar Series, December 4. http://center.serve.org/nche/downloads/webinar/csec.pdf.

Christie, N. 1986. The ideal victim. In E. A. Fattah, ed., *From crime policy to victim policy*, 17–30. London: Macmillan.

Cizmar, M., E. Conklin, and K. Hinman. 2011. Real men get their facts straight. *SF Weekly*, June 29.

Clawson, H. J., and N. Dutch. 2008. *Case management and the victim of human trafficking: A critical service for client success*. Washington, D.C.: U.S. Department of Health and Human Services.

Clawson, H. J., and L. G. Grace. 2007. *Finding a path to recovery: Residential facilities for minor victims of domestic sex trafficking*. Washington, D.C.: U.S. Department of Health and Human Services.

Clements-Nolle, K., R. Marx, R. Guzman, and M. Katz. 2001. HIV prevalence, risk behaviors, health care use, and mental health status of transgender persons: Implications for public health intervention. *American Journal of Public Health* 91 (6): 915–921.

Cobbina, J. E., and S. S. Oselin. 2011. It's not only for the money: An analysis of adolescent versus adult entry into street prostitution. *Sociological Inquiry* 81 (3): 310–332.

Cohen, S. 1972. *Moral panics and folk devils: The creation of the mods and rockers*. London: MacGibbon & Kee.

Cole, J., and E. Anderson. 2013. *Sex trafficking of minors in Kentucky*. Lexington: Center on Drug and Alcohol Research, Center on Trauma and Children, University of Kentucky.

Conrad, P., and J. W. Schneider. 1980. *Deviance and medicalization: From badness to sickness*. St. Louis: C. V. Mosby,

Cook County State's Attorney's Office. 2010. Alvarez applauds governor's signature of Illinois Safe Children's Act. Press release, August 20. http://www.statesattorney.org/press_safechildrensact01.html.

County of San Diego Behavioral Health Services. 2011. *Transition age youth status report and recommendations*. San Diego: Health & Human Services Agency.

Cousart, C. 2013. Anatomy of a child sex trafficking case. Paper presented at the San Francisco Collaborative Against Human Trafficking Conference to End Child Sex Trafficking, August, San Francisco.

Covenant House. 2014. Our kids: Forced into prostitution. http://www.covenanthouse.org/homeless-kids/forced-prostitution.

Craggs, S., and R. Martens. 2010. *Rights, residence, rehabilitation: A comparative study of assessing residence options for trafficked persons*. Switzerland: International Organization for Migration.

Cree, V. E. 2008. Confronting sex trafficking: Lessons from history. *International Social Work* 51 (6): 763–776.

Croce, D. 2014. Understanding LGBTQ youth and trafficking. Paper presented at the Freedom Network Annual Conference, San Francisco, March–April.

Curtis, R., K. Terry, M. Dank, K. Dombrowski, and B. Khan. 2008. *Commercial sexual exploitation of children in New York City*. Volume 1: *The CSEC population in New York City: Size, characteristics, and needs*. New York: John Jay College of Criminal Justice.

Dang, M. 2013. Human trafficking in the United States: Slavery redefined? Master's thesis, University of California, Berkeley.

——. 2014. Outside-in: Inspiring change through collaboration. Paper presented at the Freedom Network Annual Conference, San Francisco, March–April.

Dank, M. 2014. Understanding LGBTQ youth and trafficking. Paper presented at the Freedom Network Annual Conference, San Francisco, March–April.

Davis, M. 2003. Addressing the needs of youth in transition to adulthood. *Administration & Policy in Mental Health* 30 (6): 495–509.

Decker, M. R., E. Miller, H. L. McCauley, D. J. Tancredi, R. R. Levenson, J. Waldman, P. Schoenwald, et al. 2012. Sex trade among young women attending family-planning clinics in Northern California. *International Journal of Gynaecology & Obstetrics* 117 (2): 173–177.

Dennis, J. P. 2008. Women are victims, men make choices: The invisibility of men and boys in the global sex trade. *Gender Issues* 25 (1): 11–25.

Denzin, N. K. 1990. Reading rational choice theory. *Rationality and Society* 2 (2): 172–179.

Do, T. 2014. States fighting sex trafficking with decriminalization of prostitution for minors. *ABC News*, October 8. http:www.abc2news.com/news/region/anne- arundel-county/states-fighting-sex-trafficking-with-decriminalization-of-prostitution-for-minors.

Dorsey, K. 2013. Sex worker policy south of the Mason Dixon Line. Paper presented at the Southern Harm Reduction and Drug Policy Conference, New Orleans, December.

Dougherty, D. M., L. M. Saxe, T. Cross, and N. Silverman. 1987. *Children's mental health: Problems and services*. Durham, N.C.: Duke University Press.

Duchnowski, A. J., and R. M. Friedman. 1990. Children's mental health: Challenges for the nineties. *Journal of Mental Health Administration* 17:3–12.

Durbar Mahila Samanwaya Committee (DMSC). 2013. *Community led anti-trafficking and child protection program*. Kolkata, India: DMSC.

Edwards, J. M., B. J. Iritani, and D. D. Hallfors. 2006. Prevalence and correlates of exchanging sex for drugs or money among adolescents in the United States. *Sexually Transmitted Infections* 82 (5): 354–358.

Egelko, B. 2015. State won't appeal ruling on sex offender tracking. *San Francisco Chronicle*, February 11. http://www.sfchronicle.com/news/article/State-AG-won-t-appeal-sex-offender-provision-6075764.php.

Elder, G. H. 1994. Time, human agency, and social change: Perspectives on the life course. *Social Psychology Quarterly* 57 (1): 4–15.

——. 1998. The life course as developmental theory. *Child Development* 69 (1): 1–12.

Estes, R. J., and N. A. Weiner. 2005. The commercial sexual exploitation of children in the United States. In S. W. Cooper, R. J. Estes, A. P. Giardino, N. D. Kellogg, and V. I. Vieth, eds., *Medical, legal, and social science aspects of child sexual exploitation: A comprehensive review of pornography, prostitution, and Internet crimes*, 95–128. St. Louis: GW Medical

Farrow, J. A., R. W. Deisher, R. Brown, J. W. Kulig, and M. D. Kipke. 1992. Health and health needs of homeless and runaway youth. A position paper of the Society for Adolescent Medicine. *Journal of Adolescent Health* 13 (8): 717–726.

Fedina, L. 2014. Use and misuse of research in books on sex trafficking: Implications for interdisciplinary researchers, practitioners, and advocates. *Trauma, Violence, & Abuse* 16 (2): 188–198.

Fine, M., N. Freudenberg, Y. Payne, T. Perkins, K. Smith, and K. Wanzer. 2003. "Anything can happen with police around": Urban youth evaluate strategies of surveillance in public places. *Journal of Social Issues* 59 (1): 141–158.

Finkelhor, D., and R. Ormrod. 2004. *Prostitution of juveniles: Patterns from NIBRS*. Washington, D.C.: Office of Juvenile Justice and Delinquency Prevention, U.S. Department of Justice.

Finklea, K., A. Fernandes-Alcantara, and A. Siskin. 2011. *Sex trafficking of children in the United States: Overview and issues for Congress*. Washington, D.C.: Congressional Research Service.

Fong, R., and J. B. Cardoso. 2010. Child human trafficking victims: Challenges for the child welfare system. *Evaluation and Program Planning* 33 (3): 311–316.

French, M. 2013. Anatomy of a child sex trafficking case. Paper presented at the San Francisco Collaborative Against Human Trafficking Conference to End Child Sex Trafficking, San Francisco, August.

Frensch, K., and G. Cameron. 2002. Treatment of choice or a last resort? A review of residential mental health placements for children and youth. *Child and Youth Care Forum* 31 (5): 307–339.

Friedman, S. A. 2013. *And boys too: An ECPAT-USA discussion paper about the lack of recognition of the commercial sexual exploitation of boys in the United States*. New York: ECPAT-USA.

Garofalo, R., J. Deleon, E. Osmer, M. Doll, and G. W. Harper. 2006. Overlooked, misunderstood, and at-risk: Exploring the lives and HIV risk of ethnic minority male-to-female transgender youth. *Journal of Adolescent Health* 38 (3): 230–236.

Garringer, M. 2005. *Delivering quality mentoring services in rural and tribal settings: A case study of the North Dakota tribal rural mentoring partnership*. Mentoring Resource Center Case Study Series. Folsom, Calif.: U.S. Department of Education Mentoring Resource Center.

Gelles, R. J. 1980. Violence in the family: A review of research in the seventies. *Journal of Marriage and Family* 42 (4): 873–885.

Gibbons, D., P. Lichtenberg, and J. van Beusekom. 1994. Working with victims: Being emphatic helpers. *Clinical Social Work Journal* 22 (2): 211–222.

Glaser, B., and A. Strauss. 1967. *The discovery of grounded theory: Strategies for qualitative research.* Chicago: Aldine Transaction.

Glisson, C., and M. Durick. 1988. Predictors of job satisfaction and organizational commitment in human services organizations. *Administrative Science Quarterly* 33 (1): 61–81.

Glisson, C., and A. Hemmelgarn. 1998. The effects of organizational climate and interorganizational coordination on the quality and outcomes of children's service systems. *Child Abuse & Neglect* 22 (5): 401–421.

Glisson, C., and L. James. 1992. The interorganizational coordination of services to children in state custody. *Administration in Social Work* 16 (3–4): 65–80.

Godette, D. C., S. Headen, and C. L. Ford. 2006. Windows of opportunity: Fundamental concepts for understanding alcohol-related disparities experienced by young blacks in the United States. *Prevention Science* 7 (4): 377–387.

Goff, P. A., M. J. William, J. Eberhardt, and M. C. Jackson. 2008. Not yet human: Implicit knowledge, historical dehumanization, and contemporary consequences. *Journal of Personality and Social Psychology* 94 (2): 292–306.

Goldman, J., M. K. Salus, D. Woldott, and K. Y. Kennedy. 2003. *A coordinated response to child abuse and neglect: The foundation for practice.* Child Abuse and Neglect User Manual Series. Washington, D.C.: Administration for Children and Families, U.S. Department of Health and Human Services.

Goodman, L. A., K. F. Smyth, A. M. Borges, and R. Singer. 2009. When crises collide: How intimate partner violence and poverty intersect to shape women's mental health and coping. *Trauma Violence Abuse* 10 (4): 306–329.

Gottfredson, M. R., and D. M. Gottfredson. 1988. *Decision making in criminal justice: Toward the rational exercise of discretion.* 2nd ed. New York: Plenum.

Grace, L. G., M. Starck, J. Potenza, P. A. Kenney, and A. H. Sheetz. 2012. Commercial sexual exploitation of children and the school nurse. *Journal of School Nursing* 28 (6): 410–417.

Gragg, F., I. Petta, H. Bernstein, K. Eisen, and L. Quinn. 2007. *New York prevalence study of commercially sexually exploited children.* Rockville, Md.: WESTAT.

Grant, J. M., L. A. Mottet, J. Tanis, J. Harrison, J. L. Herman, and M. Keisling. 2011. *Injustice at every turn: A report of the national transgender discrimination survey.* Washington, D.C.: National Center for Transgender Equality and National Gay and Lesbian Task Force.

Gray, D. 1973. Turning-out: A study of teenage prostitution. *Journal of Contemporary Ethnography* 1:401–425.

Greene, J. M., S. T. Ennett, C. L. Ringwalt. 1999. Prevalence and correlates of survival sex among runaway and homeless youth. *American Journal of Public Health* 89 (9): 1406–1409.

Greene, M. B. 1993. Chronic exposure to violence and poverty: Interventions that work for youth. *Crime & Delinquency* 39 (1): 106–124.

Greer, C. 2007. News media, victims, and crime. In P. Davies, P. Francis, and C. Greer, eds., *Victims, crime, and society*, 20–49. London: Sage.

Grittner, F. K. 1990. *White slavery: Myth, ideology, and American law*. New York: Garland.

Haley, N., E. Roy, P. Leclerc, J. F. Boudreau, and J. F. Boivin. 2004. HIV risk profile of male street youth involved in survival sex. *Sexually Transmitted Infections* 80 (6): 526–530.

Halter, S. 2010. Factors that influence police conceptualizations of girls involved in prostitution in six U.S. cities: Child sexual exploitation victims or delinquents? *Child Maltreatment* 15 (2): 152–160.

Hanna, C. 2002. Somebody's daughter: The domestic sex trafficking of girls for the commercial sex industry and the power of love. *William & Mary Journal of Women and the Law* 9 (1): 1–29.

Harris, J., S. Scott, and P. Skidmore. 2006. *Child sexual exploitation: A Barnardo's teaching case on the integration of practice, research, and policy*. Barkinside, U.K.: Barnardo's.

Hess, A. 2014. Most of what you think you know about sex trafficking isn't true. *Slate*, April 23. http://www.slate.com/blogs/xx_factor/2014/04/23/study_of_sex_workers_and_pimps_reveals_how_the_market_for_underage_sex_actually.html.

Hodge, D. 2008. Sexual trafficking in the United States: A domestic problem with transnational dimensions. *Social Work* 53 (2): 143–152.

Hodges, S., T. Nesman, and M. Hernandez. 1999. *Promising practices: Building collaboration in systems of care*. Systems of Care: Promising Practices in Children's Mental Health, 1998 series, vol. 6. Washington, D.C.: Center for Effective Collaboration and Practice, American Institutes for Research.

Holden, S. 2013. Movie review: True story inspires tale of sex trade; in a twist, a U.S. marshal is the bad guy. *New York Times*, March 19. http://www.nytimes.com/2013/03/20/movies/eden-depicts-sex-trafficking-in-the-united-states.html?gwt=pay&_r=0.

Holstein, J. A., and G. Miller. 1990. Rethinking victimization: An interactional approach to victimology. *Symbolic Interaction* 13 (1): 103–122.

Horning, A. 2013. Peeling the onion: Domestically trafficked minors and other sex work involved youth. *Dialectical Anthropology* 37:299–307.

Horwath, J., and T. Morrison. 2007. Collaboration, integration, and change in children's services: Critical issues and key ingredients. *Child Abuse & Neglect* 31 (1): 55–69.

Huxham, C., and S. Vaugen. 2000. Ambiguity, complexity, and dynamics in the membership of collaboration. *Human Relations* 53 (6): 771–806.

Illback, R. J., and T. K. Neill. 1995. Service coordination in mental health systems for children, youth, and families: Progress, problems, prospects. *Journal of Mental Health Administration* 22 (1): 17–28.

Iman, J., C. Fullwood, N. Paz, D. W, and S. Hassan. 2009. *Girls do what they have to do to survive: Illuminating methods used by girls in the sex trade and street economy to fight back and heal*. Chicago: Young Women's Empowerment Project.

Institute of Medicine and National Research Council. 2013. *Confronting commercial sexual exploitation and sex trafficking of minors in the United States*. Washington, D.C.: National Academies Press.

International Human Rights Clinic. 2013. *Troubling gaps in the U.S. response to human trafficking under the International Covenant on Civil and Political Rights.* Santa Clara, Calif.: Santa Clara University School of Law.

Jana, S., B. Dey, S. Reza-Paul, and R. Steen. 2013. Combating human trafficking in the sex trade: Can sex workers do it better? *Journal of Public Health* (Oxford) 36 (4): 622–628.

Jekowsky, L. 2014. Un-safe harbor: Why U.S. state legislation is ineffectively addressing sex trafficking of minors. Human Trafficking Center, March 10. http://humantraffickingcenter.org/posts-by-htc-associates/un-safe-harbor-why-u-s-state-legislation-is-ineffectively-addressing-sex-trafficking-of-minors/.

Jesson, J. 1993. Understanding adolescent female prostitution: A literature review. *Journal of Social Work* 23 (5): 517–530.

Johnson, L. J., D. Zorn, B. K. Y. Tam, M. Lamontagne, and S. A. Johnson. 2003. Stakeholders' views of factors that impact successful interagency collaboration. *Exceptional Children* 69 (2): 195–209.

Kaestle, C. E. 2012. Selling and buying sex: A longitudinal study of risk and protective factors in adolescence. *Prevention Science* 13 (3): 314–322.

Kagan, S. L. 1993. *Integrating services for children and families: Understanding the past to shape the future.* New Haven, Conn.: Yale University Press.

Kaye, R. 2007. Invisible chains: Sex slavery in the U.S. *Anderson Cooper 360*, CNN, January 24. http://transcripts.cnn.com/TRANSCRIPTS/0701/24/acd.01.html.

Kennedy, M. A., C. Klein, J. T. K. Bristowe, B. S. Copper, and J. C. Yuille. 2007. Routes and recruitment: Pimps' techniques and other circumstances that lead to street prostitution. *Journal of Aggression, Maltreatment & Trauma* 15 (2): 1–19.

Kennedy, M. A., and N. J. Pucci. 2007. *Las Vegas rapid assessment: The identification and delivery of services to domestic minor sex trafficking victims in Las Vegas, Nevada.* Arlington, Va.: Shared Hope International.

Khan, H. 2010. Child sex trafficking growing in the U.S.: "I got my childhood taken from me." *ABC News*, May 5. http://abcnews.go.com/US/domestic-sex-trafficking-increasing-united-states/story?id=10557194.

Kliner, M., and L. Stroud. 2012. Psychological and health impact of working with victims of sex trafficking. *Journal of Occupational Health* 54 (1): 9–15.

Koepplin, S., and A. Pierce. 2009. *Commercial sexual exploitation of American Indian women and girls.* Lincoln: University of Nebraska Press.

Konstantopoulos, M. W., R. Ahn, E. J. Alpert, E. Cafferty, A. McGahan, T. P. Williams, J. P. Castor, et al. 2013. An international comparative public health analysis of sex trafficking of women and girls in eight cities: Achieving a more effective health sector response. *Journal of Urban Health* 90 (6): 1194–1204.

Kotrla, K. 2010. Domestic minor sex trafficking in the United States. *Social Work* 55 (2): 181–187.

Kovtun, R. 2013. Anti-trafficking laws and other ways to combat modern slavery: Ambassador Luis CdeBaca offers insights. *MinnPost*, November 25. http://www.minnpost.com/minnpost-asks/2013/11/anti-trafficking-laws-and-other-ways-combat-modern-slavery-ambassador-luis-cde.

Koyama, E. 2011a. *Understanding the complexities of sex work/trade and trafficking.* Portland, Ore.: Confluere.

——. 2011b. *War on terror & war on trafficking.* Portland, Ore.: Confluere.

——. 2014. Collateral damage: Sex workers and anti-trafficking campaigns. Paper presented at the Freedom Network Annual Conference, San Francisco, March–April.

Kramer, L. A., and E. C. Berg. 2003. A survival analysis of timing of entry into prostitution: The differential impact of race, educational level, and childhood/adolescent risk factors. *Sociological Inquiry* 73 (4): 511–528.

Kristof, N. 2011. What about American girls sold on the streets? *New York Times*, April 24. http://www.nytimes.com/2011/04/24/opinion/24kristof.html.

——. 2013. Chipping away at sex trafficking in America. *New York Times*, October 12. http://kristof.blogs.nytimes.com/2013/10/12/chipping-away-at-sex-trafficking-in-america/?_php=true&_type=blogs&_r=0&assetType=opinion.

——. 2014. When Emily was sold for sex. *New York Times*, February 12. http://www.nytimes.com/2014/02/13/opinion/kristof-when-emily-was-sold-for-sex.html?&assetType=opinion.

Kurtz, P. D., E. Lindsey, S. Jarvis, N. Williams, and L. Nackerud. 2000. How runaway and homeless youth navigate troubled waters: Personal strengths and resources. *Child and Adolescent Social Work Journal* 17 (2): 381–402.

Lamb, S. 1999. Constructing the victim: Popular images and lasting labels. In S. Lamb, ed., *New versions of victims: Feminists struggle with the concept*, 108–138. New York: New York University Press.

Lerman, M. 2014. Understanding LGBTQ youth and trafficking. Paper presented at the Freedom Network Annual Conference, San Francisco, March–April.

Lew, C. 2012. *Sex trafficking of domestic minors in Phoenix, Arizona: A research project.* Scottsdale, Ariz.: Diane & Bruce Halle Foundation.

Lin, A. C. 2000. *Reform in the making: The implementation of social policy in prison.* Princeton, N.J.: Princeton University Press.

Lipsky, M. 1980. *Street-level bureaucracy: Dilemmas of the individual in public services.* New York: Russell Sage.

Lloyd, R. 2012. Urban legends and hoaxes: How hyperbole hurts trafficking victims. *Huffington Post*, February 3. http://www.huffingtonpost.com/rachel-lloyd/village-voice-escort-ads_b_1250617.html.

Locke, C. 2014. Woman arrested in Roseville accused of prostitution, using teen as pimp. *Sacramento Bee*, May 20. http://www.sacbee.com/2014/05/20/6420205/woman-arrested-in-roseville-accused.html#storylink=cpy.

Loken, G. 1986. The federal battle against child sexual exploitation: Proposals for reform. *Harvard Women's Law Journal* 9:105–134.

Loseke, D. R., and E. Cahill. 1984. The social construction of deviance: Experts on battered women. *Social Problems* 31:296–310.

Lundman, R. J. 1996a. Demeanor and arrest: Additional evidence from previously unpublished data. *Journal of Research in Crime & Delinquency* 33:306–323.

———. 1996b. Extralegal variables and arrest. *Journal of Research in Crime and Delinquency* 33:349–353.

Lutnick, A., and D. Cohan. 2008. Working conditions, HIV, STIs, and hepatitis C among female sex workers in San Francisco, CA. Paper presented at the International AIDS Conference, Mexico City, August.

Lutnick, A., J. Harris, J. Lorvick, H. Cheng, L. D. Wenger, P. Bourgois, and A. H. Kral. 2014. Examining the associations between sex trade involvement, rape, and symptomatology of sexual abuse trauma. *Journal of Interpersonal Violence* (advance publication online). doi: 10.1177/0886260514549051.

Lynch, D., and K. Widner. 2008. *Commercial sexual exploitation of children in Georgia: Service delivery and legislative recommendations for state and local policy makers.* Atlanta: Barton Child Law and Policy Clinic.

Lynch, J., and G. D. Smith. 2005. A life course approach to chronic disease epidemiology. *Annual Review of Public Health* 26:1–35.

Manteuffel, B., R. L. Stephens, and R. Santiago. 2002. Overview of the national evaluation of the comprehensive community mental health services for children and their families program and summary of current findings. *Children's Services: Social Policy, Research, & Practice* 5 (1): 3–20.

Marcus, A., and R. Curtis. 2013. Implementing policy for invisible populations: Social work and social policy in a federal anti-trafficking taskforce in the United States. *Social Policy and Society*, FirstView, 1–12. doi: 10.1017/S1474746413000304.

Marcus, A., A. Horning, R. Curtis, J. Sanson, and E. Thompson. 2014. Conflict and agency among sex workers and pimps: A closer look at domestic minor sex trafficking. *ANNALS of the American Academy of Political and Social Science* 653 (1): 225–246.

Marcus, A., R. Riggs, A. Horning, R. Curtis, S. Rivera, and E. Thompson. 2011. *Is child to adult as victim is to criminal? Social policy and street-based sex work in the United States.* Working Paper Series 02. New York: Social Networks Research Group.

Marshall, B. D. L., K. Shannon, T. Kerr, R. Zhang, and E. Wood. 2010. Survival sex work and increased HIV risk among sexual minority street-involved youth. *Journal of Acquired Immune Deficiency Syndromes* 53 (5): 661–664.

Martin, L., M. O. Hearst, and R. Widome. 2010. Meaningful differences: Comparison of adult women who first traded sex as a juvenile versus as an adult. *Violence Against Women* 16 (11): 1252–1269.

Mason, F. 2013. Providing services to runaway youth and victims of human trafficking. Office for Victims of Crime Provider Forum Webinar Series, January 22. http://ovc.ncjrs.gov/ovcproviderforum/asp/sub.asp?Topic_ID=183.

McClanahan, S. F., G. M. McClelland, K. M. Abram, and L. A. Teplin. 1999. Pathways into prostitution among female jail detainees and their implications for mental health services. *Psychiatric Services* 50 (12): 1606–1613.

McEachern, A. W., and R. Bauzer. 1967. Factors related to disposition in juvenile police contacts. In M. W. Klein, ed., *Juvenile gangs in context*, 148–160. Englewood Cliffs, N.J.: Prentice-Hall.

McLemore, M. 2012. *Sex workers at risk: Condoms as evidence of prostitution in four US cities.* Washington, D.C.: Human Rights Watch.

——. 2013. *In harm's way: State response to sex workers, drug users, and HIV in New Orleans.* Washington, D.C.: Human Rights Watch.

Medina, A. 2014. Understanding LGBTQ youth and trafficking. Paper presented at the Freedom Network Annual Conference, San Francisco, March–April.

Meisner, T. G. 2009. Shifting the paradigm from prosecution to protection of child victims of prostitution. *Journal of the National District Attorneys Association* 43 (2): 22–24.

Meyers, M. K. 1993. Organizational factors in the integration of services for children. *Social Service Review* 67 (4): 547–575.

Miller, C. L., S. J. Fielden, M. W. Tyndall, R. Zhang, K. Gibson, and K. Shannon. 2011. Individual and structural vulnerability among female youth who exchange sex for survival. *Journal of Adolescent Health* 49 (1): 36–41.

Mitchell, K. J., D. Finkelhor, and J. Wolak. 2010. Conceptualizing juvenile prostitution as child maltreatment: Findings from the National Juvenile Prostitution Study. *Child Maltreatment* 15 (1): 18–36.

Mitchell, K. J., L. M. Jones, D. Finkelhor, and J. Wolak. 2011. Internet-facilitated commercial sexual exploitation of children: Findings from a nationally representative sample of law enforcement agencies in the United States. *Sexual Abuse: A Journal of Research and Treatment* 23 (1): 43–71.

Moffitt, T. E. 1993. Adolescence-limited and life-course-persistent antisocial behavior: A developmental taxonomy. *Psychological Review* 100 (4): 674–701.

Mogulesco, K. 2014. Justice and dignity for survivors through vacating convictions. Paper presented at the Freedom Network Annual Conference, San Francisco, March–April.

Moore, J. 2005. *Unaccompanied and homeless youth: Review of literature (1995–2005).* Greensboro, N.C.: National Center for Homeless Education.

Morash, M. 1984. Establishment of a juvenile police record: The influence of individual and peer group characteristics. *Criminology* 22:97–111.

Mukasey, M. B., C. K. Daley, and D. W. Hagy. 2007. *Commercial sexual exploitation of children: What do we know and what do we do about it?* Washington, D.C.: National Institute of Justice, U.S. Department of Justice.

Musto, J. 2013. Domestic minor sex trafficking and the detention-to-protection pipeline. *Dialectical Anthropology* 37:257–276.

Nadon, S. M., C. Koverola, and E. H. Schludermann. 1998. Antecedents to prostitution. *Journal of Interpersonal Violence* 13 (2): 206–221.

Nixon, K., L. Tutty, P. Downe, K. Gorkoff, and J. Ursel. 2002. The everyday occurrence: Violence in the lives of girls exploited through prostitution. *Violence Against Women* 8 (9): 1016–1043.

O'Connell Davidson, J. 1998. *Prositution, power, and freedom.* Cambridge: Polity Press.

——. 2005. *Children in the global sex trade.* Cambridge: Polity Press.

Perlberg, A. 2011. The continued dehumanization of blacks. *Gender News*, July 31. http://gender.stanford.edu/news/2011/continued-dehumanization-blacks#sthash .iZ6Ci37O.8L7tmQV6.dpuf.

Pfohl, S. 1994. *Images of deviance and social control: A sociological history.* New York: McGraw Hill.

Phillips, S., C. Coates, C. Ortiz, L. Rast, J. Sheltry, and K. Thomas. 2014. *Clearing the slate: Seeking effective remedies for criminalized trafficking victims.* New York: School of Law, City University of New York.

Phoenix, J. 2002. In the name of protection: Youth prostitution policy reforms in England and Wales. *Critical Social Policy* 22:353–375.

Pierce, A. S. 2012. American Indian adolescent girls: Vulnerability to sex trafficking, intervention strategies. *American Indian and Alaska Native Mental Health Research* 19 (1): 37–56.

Pinto, N. 2011. Weird science: How a bogus sex trafficking study fooled some of the most respected media outlets in the country. *SF Weekly*, March 23, 11–16.

Pollio, D. E., S. J. Thompson, L. Tobias, D. Reid, and E. Spitznagel. 2006. Longitudinal outcomes for youth receiving runaway/homeless shelter services. *Journal of Youth and Adolescence* 35 (5): 852–859.

Preventing Sex Trafficking and Strengthening Families Act. 2014. Pub. L. No. 113-183. https://www.congress.gov/bill/113th-congress/house-bill/4980/text.

Pupovac, J. 2013. Feds recast child prostitutes as victims, not criminals. *NPR*, October 24. http://www.npr.org/2013/10/24/240493177/feds-recast-child-prostitutes-as-victims-not-criminals?sc=17&f=1001.

Quinney, R. 1972. Who is the victim? *Criminology* 10 (3): 314–323.

Quintana, N. S., J. Rosenthal, and J. Krehely. 2010. *On the streets: The federal response to gay and transgender youth.* Washington, D.C.: Center for American Progress.

Raphael, J., and B. Myers-Powell. 2010. *From victims to victimizers: Interviews with 25 ex-pimps in Chicago.* Chicago: Schiller DuCanto and Fleck Family Law Center, DePaul University College of Law.

Raphael, J., J. Reichert, and M. Powers. 2010. Pimp control and violence: Domestic sex trafficking of Chicago women and girls. *Women & Criminal Justice* 20 (1–2): 89–104.

Raphael, J., and D. Shapiro. 2002. *Sisters speak out: The lives and needs of prostituted women in Chicago. A research study.* Chicago: Center for Impact Research. http://www.impactresearch.org/documents/sistersspeakout.pdf.

Ray, N. 2006. *Lesbian, gay, bisexual, and transgender youth: An epidemic of homelessness.* New York: National Gay and Lesbian Task Force Policy Institute and the National Coalition for the Homeless.

Reid, J. A. 2010. Doors wide shut: Barriers to the successful delivery of victim services for domestically trafficked minors in a southern U.S. metropolitan area. *Women & Criminal Justice* 20 (1): 147–166.

———. 2012. Rapid assessment exploring impediments to successful prosecutions of sex traffickers of U.S. minors. *Journal of Police and Criminal Psychology*, Online First™, June 23, 2012. doi: 10.1007/s11896-012-9106-6.

Richardson, J. 2014. Is sexual abuse to blame for trafficking? http://jesrichardson.com/is-sexual-abuse-to-blame-for-trafficking/.

Richardson, R. 2014. Justice and dignity for survivors through vacating convictions. Paper presented at the Freedom Network Annual Conference, San Francisco, March–April.

Rivard, J. C., and J. P. Morrissey. 2003. Factors associated with interagency coordination in a child mental health service system demonstration. *Administration and Policy in Mental Health and Mental Health Services Research* 30 (5): 397–415.

Rose, K. 2014. Plenary: Update on the federal strategic action plan on services for victims of human trafficking in the United States. Paper presented at the Freedom Network Annual Conference, San Francisco, March–April.

Saar, M. S. 2010. Girl slavery in America. *Huffington Post*, June 20. http://www.huffingtonpost.com/malika-saada-saar/girl-slavery-in-america_b_544978.html.

Saunders, P. 2005. Identity to acronym: How "child prostitution" became "CSEC." In E. Bernstein and L. Schaffner, eds., *Regulating sex: The politics of intimacy and identity*, 167–185. New York: Routledge.

Schaffner, L. 2006. *Girls in trouble with the law*. New Brunswick, N.J.: Rutgers University Press.

Schneir, A., N. Stefanidis, C. Mounier, D. Ballin, D. Gailey, H. Carmichael, and T. Battle. 2007. Trauma among homeless youth. *National Child Traumatic Stress Network Culture and Trauma Brief* 2 (1): 1–7.

Schur, E. M. 1965. *Crimes without victims: Deviant behavior and public policy: Abortion, homosexuality, and drug addiction*. Upper Saddle River, N.J.: Prentice-Hall.

Schwartz, S. 2009. Harboring concerns: The problematic conceptual reorientation of juvenile prostitution adjudication in New York. *Columbia Journal of Gender and Law* 18 (1): 235–246.

Schweig, S. 2012. Changing perceptions: A conversation on prostitution diversion with Judge Fernando Camacho. February 4. http://www.courtinnovation.org/research/changing-perceptions-conversation-prostitution-diversion-judge-fernando-camacho-0.

Sevelius, J. 2009. "There's no pamphlet for the kind of sex I have": HIV-related risk factors and protective behaviors among transgender men who have sex with nontransgender men. *Journal of the Association of Nurses in AIDS Care* 20 (5): 398–410.

Shannon, K., T. Kerr, B. Marshall, K. Li, R. Zhang, S. A. Strathdee, M. W. Tyndall, J. G. Mantaner, and E. Wood. 2010. Survival sex work involvement as a primary risk factor for hepatitis C virus acquisition in drug-using youths in a Canadian setting. *Archives of Pediatrics & Adolescent Medicine* 164 (1): 61–65.

Shaw, R. 2010. Human trafficking in Kentucky. On *Connections with Renee Shaw*, KET television, Louisville, Ky., February 5. http://www.ket.org/cgi-bin/cheetah/watch_video.pl?nola=KCWRS+000520.

——. 2012. Sexual assault/human trafficking. On *Connections with Renee Shaw*, KET television, Louisville, Ky., February 24. http://www.ket.org/cgi-bin/cheetah/watch_video.pl?nola=KCWRS+000722&altdir=&template=.

——. 2013. Human trafficking. On *Connections with Renee Shaw*, KET television, Louisville, Ky., November 15. http://www.ket.org/cgi-bin/cheetah/watch_video.pl?nola=KCWRS+000911.

Sherman, F. T. 2012. Justice for girls: Are we making progress? *UCLA Law Review* 59:1584–1628.

Sims, E. D. 2012. Law enforcement and social service responses to human trafficking in Marin County. Master's thesis, Sonoma State University.

Smith, B. D., and S. E. F. Donovan. 2003. Child welfare practice in organizational and institutional context. *Social Science Review* 77 (4): 541–563.

Smith, L., S. H. Vardaman, and M. Snow. 2009. *The national report on domestic minor sex trafficking: America's prostituted children*. Arlington, Va.: Shared Hope International.

Soloman, E. E. 1986. Private and public sector managers: An empirical investigation of job characteristics and organizational climate. *Journal of Applied Psychology* 71:247–259.

State of California Department of Justice. 2014. Criminal justice profiles: Interactive crime statistics tables. Data file. http://oag.ca.gov/crime/cjsc/stats/arrests.

Stewart, D. 2013. Providing services to runaway youth and victims of human trafficking. Office for Victims of Crime Provider Forum Webinar Series, January 22. http://ovc.ncjrs.gov/ovcproviderforum/asp/sub.asp?Topic_ID=183.

Stoltz, J. M., K. Shannon, T. Kerr, R. Zhang, J. Montaner, and E. Wood. 2007. Associations between childhood maltreatment and sex work in a cohort of drug-using youth. *Social Science & Medicine* 65 (6): 1214–1221.

Stransky, M., and D. Finkelhor. 2008. *How many juveniles are involved in prostitution in the U.S.?* Durham, N.H.: Crimes Against Children Research Center.

Strauss, A., and J. Corbin. 1988. *Basics of qualitative research: Techniques and procedures for developing grounded theory*. 2nd ed. Thousand Oaks: Sage Publications.

Stroul, B., and R. Friedman. 1986. *A system of care children and youth with severe emotional disturbances*. Rev. ed. Washington, D.C.: Child Development Center, Georgetown University.

Stroul, B. A., S. A. Pires, M. I. Armstrong, and S. Zaro. 2002. The impact of managed care on systems of care that serve children with serious emotional disturbances and their families. *Children's Services: Social Policy, Research & Practice* 5 (1): 21–36.

Sutherland, E. H. 1934. *Principles of criminology*. Philadelphia: Lippincott.

Szasz, T. S. 2001. *Pharmacracy: Medicine and politics in America*. Westport, Conn.: Praeger.

Tiapula, S. L., and A. Turkel. 2008. Identifying the victims of human trafficking. *Journal of the National District Attorneys Association* 42 (2): 10–15.

Tittle, C. R. 1969. Crime rates and legal sanctions. *Social Problems* 16 (4): 409–423.

Torres, C. A., and N. Paz. 2012. *Bad encounter line: A participatory action research project*. Chicago: Young Women's Empowerment Project.

Trafficking Victims Protection Reauthorization Act. 2003. Pub L. No. 108-913. http://www.state.gov/j/tip/laws/61130.htm.

——. 2005. Pub. L. No. 109-164. http://www.state.gov/j/tip/laws/61106.htm.

——. 2013. Pub. L. No. 113-4. http://www.gpo.gov/fdsys/pkg/PLAW-113publ4/html/PLAW-113publ4.htm.

Tucker, J. 2013. Oakland schools' mission to end child trafficking. *San Francisco Chronicle*, December 20. http://www.sfgate.com/crime/article/Oakland-schools-mission-to-end-child-trafficking-5080256.php.

Turner, R. B. 2014. How not to talk about human trafficking. Human Trafficking Center, January 21. http://humantraffickingcenter.org/posts-by-htc-associates/how-not-to-talk-about-human-trafficking/.

Tyler, K. A., D. R. Hoyt, and L. B. Whitbeck. 2000. The effects of early sexual abuse on later sexual victimization among female homeless and runaway adolescents. *Journal of Interpersonal Violence* 15 (3): 235–250.

Ungar, M. 2005a. Pathways to resilience among children in child welfare, corrections, mental health, and educational settings: Navigation and negotiation. *Child and Youth Care Forum* 34 (6): 423–444.

———. 2005b. Resilience among children in child welfare, corrections, mental health, and educational settings: Recommendations for service. *Child and Youth Care Forum* 34 (6): 445–464.

Unger, J. B., T. R. Simon, T. L. Newman, S. B. Montgomery, M. D. Kipke, and M. Albomoz. 1998. Early adolescent street youth: An overlooked population with unique problems and service needs. *Journal of Early Adolescence* 18:325–348.

United Nations. 2000. Protocol to Prevent, Suppress, and Punish Trafficking in Persons Especially Women and Children, supplementing the United Nations Convention Against Transnational Organized Crime. https://treaties.un.org/doc/Publication/UNTS/Volume%202237/v2237.pdf.

U.S. Census Bureau. 2014. United States population by age and sex. http://www.census.gov/popclock/.

U.S. Department of Health and Human Services, Administration for Children, Youth, and Families. 2013. *Guidance to states and services on addressing human trafficking of children and youth in the United States*. Washington, D.C.: U.S. Department of Health and Human Services.

U.S. Department of State. 2010. *Trafficking in persons report*. 10th ed. Washington, D.C.: U.S. Department of State. http://www.state.gov/documents/organization/142979.pdf.

———. 2012. *Trafficking in persons report*. 12th ed. Washington, D.C.: U.S. Department of State. http://www.state.gov/documents/organization/192598.pdf.

U.S. Federal Bureau of Investigation (FBI). 2010a. Table 32: Ten-year arrest trends: Totals, 2000–2009. In *Crime in the United States, 2009*. https://www2.fbi.gov/ucr/cius2009/data/table_32.html.

———. 2010b. Table 33: Ten-year arrest trends, by sex: Totals, 2000–2009. In *Crime in the United States, 2009*. http://www.fbi.gov/about-us/cjis/ucr/crime-in-the-u.s/2009.

———. 2014a. Table 32: Ten-year arrest trends: Totals, 2003–2012. In *Crime in the United States, 2013*. http://www.fbi.gov/about-us/cjis/ucr/crime-in-the-u.s/2013/crime-in-the-u.s.-2013/tables/table-32/table_32_ten_year_arrest_trends_totals_2013.xls.

———. 2014b. Table 69: Arrests by state: 2013. In *Crime in the United States, 2013*. http://www.fbi.gov/about-us/cjis/ucr/crime-in-the-u.s/2013/crime-in-the-u.s.-2013/tables/table-69/table_69_arrest_by_state_2013.xls.

———. 2014c. Violent crimes against children: Innocence lost. http://www.fbi.gov/about-us/investigate/vc_majorthefts/cac/innocencelost.

——— 2015. *Human trafficking 2013 report*. Washington, D.C.: FBI. http://www.fbi.gov/about-us/cjis/ucr/human-trafficking-2013-report.

U.S. Human Rights Network International Covenant on Civil and Political Rights. 2014. *Concluding observation on the fourth periodic report of the United States of America*. Washington, D.C.: United Nations.

U.S. Senate. 2005. *Exploiting Americans on American soil: Domestic trafficking exposed. Hearing before the Commission on Security and Cooperation in Europe*. 109th Cong., 1st sess., June 7. http://digitalcommons.unl.edu/cgi/viewcontent.cgi?article=1011&context=humtraffdata.

Vanek, J. 2012. Panel discussion about Proposition 35 (the Case Act) on human trafficking in California. Freeman Spogli Institute for International Studies, Stanford University, Palo Alto, Calif., October.

Van Leeuwen, J. M., S. Boyle, S. Salomonsen-Sautel, D. N. Baker, J. T. Garcia, A. Hoffman, and C. J. Hopfer. 2006. Lesbian, gay, and bisexual homeless youth: An eight-city public health perspective. *Child Welfare* 85:151–170.

Victims of Trafficking and Violence Protection Act of 2000. 2000. Pub. L. No. 106-386. http://www.state.gov/j/tip/laws/61124.htm.

Von Hentig, H. 1948. *The criminal and his victim*. New Haven, Conn.: Yale University Press.

Walker, K. E. 2002. Exploitation of children and young people through prostitution. *Journal of Child Health Care* 6 (3): 182–188.

———. 2013a. *Ending the commercial sexual exploitation of children: A call for multi-system collaboration in California*. Sacramento: California Child Welfare Council.

———. 2013b. Nexus between child sex trafficking and domestic violence, runaways, & foster care. Paper presented at the San Francisco Collaborative Against Human Trafficking Conference to End Child Sex Trafficking, San Francisco, August.

Walker-Rodriquez, A., and R. Hill. 2011. *Human sex trafficking*. Law Enforcement Bulletin. Washington, D.C.: U.S. Federal Bureau of Investigation.

Walklate, S. 2012. Who is the victim of crime? Paying homage to the work of Richard Quinney. *Crime, Media, Culture* 8 (2): 173–184.

Walkowitz, J. R. 1980. *Prostitution and Victorian society*. Cambridge: Cambridge University Press.

Walts, K. K., S. French, H. Moore, S. Ashai. 2011. *Building a child welfare response to child trafficking*. Chicago: Center for the Human Rights of Children, Loyola University, and International Organization for Adolescents. http://www.luc.edu/media/lucedu/chrc/pdfs/BCWRHandbook2011.pdf.

Wang, D. 2014. Human trafficking in the Northwest. On *In Close*, PBS, October 16. http://video.pbs.org/video/2365348281/.

Warf, C. W., L. F. Clark, M. Desai, S. J. Rabinovitz, G. Agahi, R. Calvo, and J. Hoffmann. 2013. Coming of age on the streets: Survival sex among homeless young women in Hollywood. *Journal of Adolescence* 36 (6): 1205–1213.

Washington Coalition of Sexual Assault Programs. 2004. Homeless, runaway, & throw-away youth: Sexual victimization and the consequences of life on the street. *Research & Advocacy Digest* 7 (1): 2–3.

Weber, A. E., J. F. Boivin, L. Blais, N. Haley, and E. Roy. 2002. HIV risk profile and prostitution among female street youths. *Journal of Urban Health* 79 (4): 525–535.

——. 2004. Predictors of initiation into prostitution among female street youths. *Journal of Urban Health* 81 (4): 584–595.

Weisberg, D. K. 1984. Children of the night: The adequacy of statutory treatment of juvenile prostitution. *American Journal of Criminal Law* 12 (1): 1–67.

Wells, M., K. J. Mitchell, and K. Ji. 2012. Exploring the role of the Internet in juvenile prostitution cases coming to the attention of law enforcement. *Journal of Child Sexual Abuse* 21 (3): 327–342.

Wharf, B. 2002. *Community work approaches to child welfare*. Peterborough, Canada: Broadview.

Whetton, D. 1981. Interorganizational relations—a review of the field. *Journal of Higher Education* 52 (1): 1–28.

Whitehead, J. W. 2014. America's dirty little secret: Sex trafficking is big business. *Huffington Post*, September 30. http://www.huffingtonpost.com/john-w-whitehead/americas-dirty-little-sec_3_b_5901700.html#es_share_ended.

White Slave Traffic Act. 1910. 36 Stat. 825, chap. 395, codified as amended at 18 U.S.C. §§ 2421–2424. http://www.hawaii.edu/hivandaids/The%20Mann%20Act%20(1910).pdf.

Whittier, H. 2014. Community comes together to address human trafficking. *My Fox Houston*, July 21. http://www.myfoxhouston.com/story/26075908/community-comes-together-to-address-human-trafficking.

Widom, C. S. 1994. Childhood victimization and risk for adolescent problem behaviors. In M. E. Lamb and R. Ketterlinus, eds., *Adolescent Problem Behaviors*, 127–164. New York: Erlbaum.

William Wilberforce Trafficking Victims Protection Reauthorization Act. 2008. Pub. L. No. 110-457. http://www.state.gov/j/tip/laws/113178.htm.

Williams, L. M. 2009. Provide justice for prostituted teens: Stop arresting and prosecuting girls. In N. A. Frost, J. D. Freilich, and T. R. Clear, eds., *Contemporary issues in criminal justice policy: Policy proposals from the American Society of Criminology conference*, 227–306. Belmont, Calif.: Cengage/Wadsworth.

——. 2010. Harm and resilience among prostituted teens: Broadening our understanding of victimization and survival. *Social Policy & Society* 9 (2): 243–254.

Wilson, E., R. Garofalo, R. Harris, A. Herrick, M. Martinez, J. Martinez, and M. Belzer (Transgender Advisory Committee and the Adolescent Medicine Trials Network for HIV/AIDS Interventions). 2009. Transgender female youth and sex work: HIV risk and a comparison of life factors related to engagement in sex work. *AIDS and Behavior* 13 (5): 902–913.

Wilson, H. W., and C. S. Widom. 2010. The role of youth problem behaviors in the path from child abuse and neglect to prostitution: A prospective examination. *Journal of Research on Adolescence* 20 (1): 210–236.

Wilson, J. Q. 1975. *Thinking about crime.* New York: Basic Books.

Winshell, J. 2012. Bay Area agencies improvise tactics to battle trafficking. *SF Public Press*, February 15. http://sfpublicpress.org/news/2012-02/bay-area-agencies-improvise-tactics-to-battle-trafficking.

Wynter, S. 1992. "No humans involved": An open letter to my colleagues. *Voices of the African Diaspora* 8 (2): 42–73.

Yates, G. L., R. G. MacKenzie, J. Pennbridge, and A. Swofford. 1991. A risk profile comparison of homeless youth involved in prostitution and homeless youth not involved. *Journal of Adolescent Health* 12 (7): 545–548.

Yoder, A., D. R. Hoyt, and L. B. Whitebeck. 1998. Suicidal behavior among homeless and runaway adolescents. *Journal of Youth and Adolescence* 27 (6): 753–771.

Zimmerman, Y. C. 2013. *Other dreams of freedom: Religion, sex, and human trafficking.* New York: Oxford University Press.

Zlotnick, C., and L. Marks. 2002. Case management services at ten federally funded sites targeting homeless children and their families. *Children's Services: Social Policy, Research & Practice* 5 (2): 113–122.

INDEX

Abused and Neglected Child Reporting
Act, 84
acquaintances, as influencers, 31–32
Administration for Children, Youth, and
Families, 60
age eligibility criteria, 7–8
Albright-Byrd, Leah, 68
American Bar Association's Child
Trafficking Policy, 113
Anderson, Elizabeth, 33
arrest rates, 75–78
"at risk" descriptor, 4–5

Bagheri, Paniz, 20, 37, 53, 56–57
Baskin, Sienna, 10, 95–96
Beckman, Marlene D., 4, 9
Berliner, Lucy, 108
Best Practices Policy Project, 107
biological family, as influencers, 32–34
Birge, Eve, 74
Birkhead, Tamar R., 114–15
Bluegrass Rape Crisis Center, 120
Bottoms, Andre, 16
Bourdieu, Pierre, 121
Bridget's Dream, 68
Bronfenbrenner, Urie, 12, 49
*Building a Child Welfare Response
to Child Trafficking* report *(The
Blueprint)*, 60, 85

Burns, Tara, 81

California, 82–84, 123–24
California Assembly Bill 12, 83, 153n10
California Assembly Bill 17, 83, 152n9
California Assembly Bill 22, 83, 152n8
California Assembly Bill 35, 153n12
California Assembly Bill 90, 83, 153n11
Californians Against Sexual Exploitation
(CASE) Act, 83, 89, 91
California Penal Code, 82
Camacho, Fernando, 72, 113
Caminetti v. United States, 3
case narrative interview guide, 134–36
Castellanos, Marissa, 55
Cauce, Ana Mari, 25
CdeBaca, Luis, 91, 115
characteristics: sample, 140–48; of sex
trade, 144–46; of young people
profiles in case narratives, 147–48
Child Trafficking Policy, 113
child welfare system, 60–64
cisgender, defined, 2
"Client Service Needs and Service
Provision" form, 129
"Closing Status" form, 129
Cobbina, Jennifer, 19–20, 23
coercion, types of, 146–47
Cole, Jennifer, 33

commercial sexual exploitation. *See sex trade*
competing priorities, 72–74
Conference to End Child Sex Trafficking (2013), 24, 39, 72
Cousart, Catherine, 24, 39
crime data, 5–6
criminalization, 82–84. *See also local responses*
Croce, Deanna, 28–29
Curtis, Ric, 30–31, 40, 42, 107–108

Dalberg, Elyse, 37–38, 42, 43–44, 50, 62
Dang, Minh, 23, 33, 45, 88, 92, 109, 120–21, 133
Dank, Meredith, 15, 42–43
data forms, 128–29
data sources: qualitative, 129–33; quantitative, 128–29
Davis, Maryann, 57–58
DCFS (Department of Children and Family Services), 84–85
decriminalization, in Illinois, 84–85
Dennis, Jeffrey P., 9
Denzin, Norman, 89
Department of Children and Family Services (DCFS), 84–85
desires, compared with needs, 19
DMSC (Durbar Mahila Samanwaya Committee), 116–17
domestic minor sex trafficking, narrative of, 106–110
Donovan, Stella, 60
drug use, supporting, 19–20
Durbar Mahila Samanwaya Committee (DMSC), 116–17

Eberhardt, Jennifer, 150–51n1
ecological systems theory, 12
economic power, 118
Education, U.S. Department of, 74
Elder, Glen, 130–31

emotional needs, fulfilling, 15–16
employment needs, 101–103
Estes, Richard, 4–5

family, as influencers, 32–34
federal law, 113–14. *See also specific Acts*
Fedina, Lisa, 6
"finder's fee," 31
Finkelhor, David, 29
Fischer, Jr., Stephen G., 78
food stamps, 63–64
force: overt, 20–21; types of, 146–47
formal business relationships, 34–35
fraud, types of, 146–47
Freedom Network Conference (2014), 15, 51–52, 69, 90, 115
French, Maureen, 72
friends, as influencers, 31–32

Galloway, Alika, 58
Girls Educational & Mentoring Service, 119
Glisson, Charles, 74
global issues, 116
Godette, Dionne, 131
Goff, Phillip, 150–51n1
gorilla pimps, 38, 150–51n1
Greene, Michael, 57
guardians, as influencers, 64–65
guarding turf, 69–70

Halter, Stephanie, 79
Hanna, Cheryl, 15
Harborview Center for Sexual Assault and Traumatic Stress, 108
harm reduction techniques, 114
Harris, Kamala, 84
Health and Human Services, U.S. Department of, 55, 60
Hemmelgarn, Anthony, 74
heterogeneity, 8–13
"hidden population," 150n15

"hierarchy of victimization," 81
Holmes, Justice, 3
Holte, United States v., 3
homelessness, impact of, 16–17
homophobia, 17–19, 103–105
Horning, Amber, 29, 41
housing needs, 98–101
Hunt, Gretchen, 25

"ideal victims," 78–82
Illback, Robert, 56
Illinois, 84–85, 124–26
Illinois Safe Children Act, 84, 153n13
immediacy, sense of, 49–50
Immigration Commission, 150n8
In-Custody Peer Counseling (SAGE), 124
individual-level violence, 36–40
individual state responses, 82–87
initiation: about, 14; association of abuse
    with sex trade involvement, 21–26;
    desires compared with needs, 19; drug
    use, 19–20; fulfilling emotional needs,
    15–16; homophobia, 17–19; impact of
    homelessness, 16–17; overt force, 20–21;
    role of neglect, 15; transphobia, 17–19
Institute of Medicine, 154n3
"Intake Status" form, 129
International Committee on the Rights of
    the Child, 113
International Women's Human Rights
    Clinic, 116
intimate partners, 35–36
involvement, transitions in, 40–46

Jana, Smarajit, 117
Jekowsky, Lauren, 93
Juvenile Court Act, 84
juvenile justice system, 66–67
juvenile prostitution. See sex trade

Kentucky Association of Sexual Assault
    Programs, 25

Kentucky Rescue & Restore, 55
Koyama, Emi, 41, 69
Kurtz, P. David, 53
Kwanzaa's Northside Women's Center, 58

Larrea, Sophia, 35
law enforcement, 67–69, 115
LCT (life course theory), 11–12, 130–31
legislation: Abused and Neglected
    Child Reporting Act, 84; California
    Assembly Bill 12, 83, 153n10;
    California Assembly Bill 17, 83,
    152n9; California Assembly Bill 22,
    83, 152n8; California Assembly Bill
    35, 153n12; California Assembly Bill
    90, 83, 153n11; Californians Against
    Sexual Exploitation (CASE) Act, 83,
    89, 91; Illinois Safe Children Act, 84,
    153n13; Juvenile Court Act, 84; Mann
    Act, 2–3, 4, 150n8, 150n9, 150n10;
    New York Safe Harbour for Exploited
    Children Act (SHA), 85; Preventing
    Sex Trafficking and Strengthening
    Families Act (2014), 151n1, 153n16;
    Protection of Children Against Sexual
    Exploitation Act, 150n8; Racketeer
    Influences and Corrupt Organizations
    (RICO) Act (1970), 114; Runaway
    and Homeless Youth Act (1974), 101,
    153n2, 154n3; Trafficking Victims
    Protection Act (TVPA) (2000), 1,
    75–78; Trafficking Victims Protection
    Reauthorization Act (TVPRA) (2003,
    2005, 2008 & 2013), 1; vacatur laws,
    95, 115–16; Victims of Trafficking and
    Violence Protection Act (2000) (see
    Trafficking Victims Protection Act
    [TVPA] [2000]); Violence Against
    Women Act, 152n6; Violence Against
    Women Reauthorization Act (2013),
    149n6; White Slave Traffic Act (1910),
    2–3, 4, 150n8, 150n9, 150n10; William

Wilberforce Trafficking Victims Protection Reauthorization Act (2008), 149n5
Lerman, Magalie, 51–52, 105
LGBTQ youth, 17–19
life course theory (LCT), 11–12, 130–31
Life Skills Program (SAGE), 124
living situation, 143–44
Lloyd, Rachel, 119
local responses: about, 75, 112; aligning state and federal law, 113–14; arrest rates, 75–78; critical analysis of state response, 87–96; "ideal victims," 78–82; individual state responses, 82–87

macrosystem challenges: about, 97–98; employment needs, 101–103; homophobia, 103–105; housing needs, 98–101; narrative of domestic minor sex trafficking, 106–110; neighborhood factors, 106; transphobia, 103–105
Mann, James R., 2–3
Mann Act, 2–3, 4, 150n8, 150n9, 150n10
Marcus, Anthony, 29, 41, 107–108
Maryland Foster Youth Resource Center, 62
Mason, Fiona, 54, 55, 98
Melendez, Jackie, 61
mesosystem challenges: about, 59; absence of services, 70–71; child welfare system, 60–64; competing priorities, 72–74; guarding turf, 69–70; juvenile justice system, 66–67; parents and guardians, 64–65; police officers, 67–69
Methodist Theological School, 109
methodological process, 128–33
microsystem challenges: about, 47–49; client-identified, 48; program eligibility requirements, 55; sense of immediacy, 49–50; social desirability, 53–54; sporadic program engagement, 51–52;

staff turnover, 55–58; trust issues, 52–53; "waiting to be eighteen," 50–51
Mitchell, Kimberly, 29
model state statute, 113
modern-day slavery. See sex trade
Mogulesco, Kate, 95, 115
Myers-Powell, Brenda, 27

National Gay and Lesbian Taskforce Policy Institute, 17
National Incident-Based Reporting System (NIBRS), 6
National Longitudinal Study of Adolescent Health, 5
National Research Council, 154n3
needs, compared with desires, 19
neglect, role of, 15
neighborhood factors, 106
Neill, T. Kerby, 56
New York, 85–87, 126–27
New York Safe Harbour for Exploited Children Act (SHA), 85
NIBRS (National Incident-Based Reporting System), 6
"no humans involved" (NHI), 150–151n1

O'Connell Davidson, Julia, 27, 28
Office for Victims of Crime, 55
O'Neale, Shalita, 62
Operation Cross Country, 78
Oselin, Sharon, 19–20, 23
overt force, 20–21

Panders and Their White Slaves (Roe), 3
parents, as influencers, 64–65
partial decriminalization model, in New York, 85–87
Pearsall, Bree, 120
peers, as influencers, 31–32
person in need of supervision (PINS), 85–86

"pharmacracy," 109
Phillips, Suzannah, 68, 116
pimp, 27–28, 29, 149n2
PINS (person in need of supervision), 85–86
police officers: as influencers, 67–69, 115; as sexual abusers, 67–68
"politics of pity," 82
Preventing Sex Trafficking and Strengthening Families Act (2014), 151n1, 153n16
primary factor, 25
priorities, competing, 72–74
programs: eligibility requirements for, 55; sporadic engagement in, 51–52
prostitution, defined, 28
Protection of Children Against Sexual Exploitation Act, 150n8

qualitative analysis code list, 137–39
qualitative data sources, 129–33
quantitative data sources, 128–29
Quinney, Richard, 82

Racketeer Influences and Corrupt Organizations (RICO) Act (1970), 114
Raphael, Jody, 27
referral sources, 140–43
relationships: formal business, 34–35; third-party, 30–31
resources exchanged for sex, 146
Richardson, Jes, 25
Richardson, Robin, 90, 114
RICO (Racketeer Influences and Corrupt Organizations) Act (1970), 114
Riggin, Ron, 112
Roberts, Celia, 38
Roe, Clifford: *Panders and Their White Slaves*, 3
Rose, Kristina, 95
Runaway and Homeless Youth Act (1974), 101, 153n2, 154n3

Safe Horizon, 28–29, 54; Streetwork Project, 35, 36, 55, 61, 100, 103, 126–27, 141, 142, 148
SAGE (Standing Against Global Exploitation) Project, 10, 20–21, 36, 38, 56–57, 123–24, 141, 142, 148
Salvation Army's STOP-IT Program, 10–11, 23, 31, 36, 37–38, 64, 92, 106, 124–26, 141, 142, 148
sample characteristics, 140–48
San Francisco Collaborative Against Human Trafficking 2013 Conference to End Child Sex Trafficking, 53
San Francisco Human Services Agency, 39
SAS (Streetwise & Safe), 103
Saunders, Penelope, 107
Schneir, Arlene, 57
service needs: about, 47–49; client-identified, 48; program eligibility requirements, 55; sense of immediacy, 49–50; social desirability, 53–54; sporadic program engagement, 51–52; staff turnover, 55–58; trust issues, 52–53; "waiting to be eighteen," 50–51
services, absence of, 70–71
severe forms of trafficking in persons, 149n4
sex trade: association of abuse with involvement in, 21–26; characteristics of, 144–46; defined, 2; disengaging from, 42–43; other names for, 1–2; reengaging, 43–46; resources exchanged for, 146
sex trafficking: statistics on, 4–8, 24; versions of, 149n1. *See also sex trade and specific topics*
sexual abuse: about, 112; association with sex trade involvement, 21–26; by family members, 112; gorilla pimps and, 38, 41; by police officers, 67–68; in undercover operations, 40

sex work, 1–2, 44, 115–16, 117, 123, 149n1
Sex Workers Project (Urban Justice
 Center), 10, 90, 95–96, 114
SHA (New York Safe Harbour for
 Exploited Children Act), 85
Skelton, Jack, 100
Smith, Brenda, 60
Smith, Linda, 33
Snow, Melissa, 33
social control agents, 81
social desirability, 53–54
social power, 118
Sonagachi Research Training Institute,
 117
staff turnover, 55–58
Standing Against Global Exploitation
 (SAGE) Project, 10, 20–21, 36, 38,
 56–57, 123–24, 141, 142, 148
state law, 113–14
state response, critical analysis of, 87–96
statistics, on sex trafficking, 4–8, 24
STOP-IT Program, 10–11, 23, 31, 36, 37–38,
 64, 92, 106, 124–26, 141, 142, 148
street based, 9
Streetwise & Safe (SAS), 103
Streetwork Project, 35, 36, 55, 61, 100, 103,
 126–27, 141, 142, 148
study site information, 123–27
surrogate family, as influencers, 32–34
"survival-focused coping," 35
survival sex, 1–2, 9
Sydow, John, 88
Szasz, Thomas, 109

third parties: about, 27–30, 111, 112;
 acquaintances, 31–32; family,
 32–34; formal business relationships,
 34–35; friends, 31–32; individual-level
 violence, 36–40; intimate partners, 35–
 36; involvement in, 29, 149n2; leaving,
 40–41; peers, 31–32; transitions in
 involvement over time, 40–46

third-party relationships, 30–31
Tomatore, Suzanne, 115
trafficker, 27–28, 29, 149n2
trafficking. See sex trade
Trafficking in Persons Report, 152n4
Trafficking Victims Advocacy Project,
 95, 115
Trafficking Victims Protection Act
 (TVPA) (2000), 1, 75–78
Trafficking Victims Protection
 Reauthorization Act (TVPRA) (2003,
 2005, 2008 & 2013), 1
transgender, 2, 79–80
transphobia, 17–19, 103–105
trust issues, 52–53
turf, guarding, 69–70
TVPA (Trafficking Victims Protection
 Act) (2000), 1, 75–78

UCR (Uniform Crime Reports), 5–6, 78,
 151–52n1, 152n2
Ungar, Michael, 63
Uniform Crime Reports (UCR), 5–6, 78,
 152n2
United Nations Convention on the Rights
 of the Child, 154n4
United Nations Trafficking in Persons
 Protocol, 149n3, 152n6, 153n15
United States, Caminetti v., 3
United States v. Holte, 3
Urban Justice Center's Sex Workers
 Project, 10, 90, 95–96, 114
Urban Justice Institute, 15, 42–43
U.S. Department of Education, 74
U.S. Department of Health and Human
 Services, 55, 60

vacatur laws, 95, 115–16
Vanek, John, 89
Vardaman, Samantha, 33
Velasquez, Adrianna, 23
"victim industry," 27

victims: about, 111; defined, 2; status of, 81

Victims of Trafficking and Violence Protection Act (2000). *See* Trafficking Victims Protection Act (TVPA) (2000)

victim-villain narrative, 120

Victim-Witness Assistance Fund, 83, 84, 89

Villarin, Joean, 35

violence, individual-level, 36–40

Violence Against Women Act, 152n6

Violence Against Women Reauthorization Act (2013), 149n6

"waiting to be eighteen," 50–51

Walts, Katherine, 60

Weiner, Neil, 4–5

Westmacott, Johannah, 37, 43, 63, 101, 102, 103

white slavery. *See* sex trade

White Slave Traffic Act (1910), 2–3, 4, 150n8, 150n9, 150n10

Widom, Cathy, 22

William Wilberforce Trafficking Victims Protection Reauthorization Act (2008), 149n5

Wilson, Helen, 22

Wirsing, Erin Knowles, 31

Wolak, Janis, 29

Woodcox, Nicole, 39, 64, 106

Yoon, Nara, 49–50

Young Women's Empowerment Project, 68

Zimmerman, Yvonne, 100, 109